NOT FOR PROFIT

The Public Square Book Series

Princeton University Press

MARTHA C. NUSSBAUM

NOT FOR

WHY DEMOCRACY

Needs

THE HUMANITIES

PROFIT

PRINCETON UNIVERSITY PRESS

PRINCETON AND OXFORD

Copyright © 2010 by Princeton University Press

Published by Princeton University Press,
41 William Street, Princeton, New Jersey 08540

In the United Kingdom: Princeton University Press, 6 Oxford Street,
Woodstock, Oxfordshire OX20 1TW

press.princeton.edu

Library of Congress Cataloging-in-Publication Data

Nussbaum, Martha Craven, 1947–
Not for profit : why democracy needs the humanities /
Martha C. Nussbaum.
p. cm. — (The public square book series)
Includes bibliographical references and index.
ISBN 978-0-691-14064-3 (hardcover : alk. paper)
1. Education, Humanistic—Philosophy.
2. Democracy and education. I. Title.
LC1011.N88 2010
370.11'5—dc22   2009053897

British Library Cataloging-in-Publication Data is available

This book has been composed in Adobe Garamond Pro
with Bodoni and Futura display

Printed on acid-free paper. ∞

Printed in the United States of America

13 15 17 19 20 18 16 14 12

[H]istory has come to a stage when the moral man, the complete man, is more and more giving way, almost without knowing it, to make room for the . . . commercial man, the man of limited purpose. This process, aided by the wonderful progress in science, is assuming gigantic proportion and power, causing the upset of man's moral balance, obscuring his human side under the shadow of soul-less organization.

—Rabindranath Tagore, *Nationalism*, 1917

Achievement comes to denote the sort of thing that a well-planned machine can do better than a human being can, and the main effect of education, the achieving of a life of rich significance, drops by the wayside.

—John Dewey, *Democracy and Education*, 1915

*To Lois Goutman, Marthe Melchior, Marion Stearns,
and all my teachers at the Baldwin School*

CONTENTS

FOREWORD

Ruth O'Brien

The humanities and arts play a central role in the history of democracy, and yet today many parents are ashamed of children who study literature or art. Literature and philosophy have changed the world, but parents all over the world are more likely to fret if their children are financially illiterate than if their training in the humanities is deficient. Even at the University of Chicago's Laboratory School—the school that gave birth to philosopher John Dewey's path-breaking experiments in democratic education reform—many parents worry that their children are not being schooled enough for financial success.

In *Not for Profit*, Nussbaum alerts us to a "silent crisis" in which nations "discard skills" as they "thirst for national profit." As the arts and humanities are everywhere downsized, there is a serious erosion of the very qualities that are essential to democracy itself. Nussbaum reminds us that great educators and nation-builders understood how the arts and humanities teach children the critical thinking that is necessary for independent action and for intelligent resistance to the power of blind tradition and authority. Students of art and literature also learn to imagine the situations of others, a capacity that is essential for a successful democracy, a necessary cultivation of our "inner eyes."

Nussbaum's particular strength in *Not for Profit* lies in the manner in which she uses her capacious knowledge of philosophy and educational theory, both Western and non-Western. Drawing on Rabindranath Tagore (the Indian Nobel Prize laureate in literature, and founder of an experimental school and university) and John Dewey, as well as on Jean Jacques Rousseau, Donald Winnicott, and Ralph Ellison, she creates a "human development model" of education, arguing that it is indispensable for democracy and for cultivating a globally minded citizenry.

The humanities and arts contribute to the development of young children at play as well as that of university students. Nussbaum argues that even the play of young children is educational, showing children how they can get along with others without maintaining total control. It connects "experiences of vulnerability and surprise to curiosity and wonder, rather than anxiety." These experiences are then extended and deepened by a wise humanities curriculum.

"[D]eficiencies in compassion," Nussbaum elaborates, "can hook up with the pernicious dynamic of disgust and shame . . . [and] shame is a universal response to human helplessness." Societies that inculcate "the myth of total control" rather than "mutual need and interdependency" only magnify this dynamic. She suggests that we think like Rousseau, who knew that his Emile must learn to identify with common human predicaments. He must see the world through the lens of many types of vulnerability, cultivating a rich imagination. Only then will he truly see people as real and equal. Only then can he be an equal among equals, understanding interdependency, as democracy and global citizenship both require. A democracy filled with citizens who lack empathy will inevitably breed more types of marginalization and stigmatization, thus exacerbating rather than solving its problems.

In *Not for Profit* Nussbaum undercuts the idea that education is primarily a tool of economic growth. She argues that economic growth does not invariably generate better quality of life. Neglect and scorn for the arts and humanities puts the quality of all our lives, and the health of our democracies, at risk.

Not for Profit is especially appropriate for this series, The Public Square. It offers readers a "call to action" in the form of a plan that replaces an educational model that undercuts democracy with one that promotes it. It builds a convincing, if at first counterintuitive, case that the very foundation of citizenship—not to mention national success—rests on the humanities and arts. We neglect them at our peril.

Nussbaum enters The Public Square with this far-reaching and expansive book, which shows us the importance of learning to play well with others—and then how to think for ourselves.

ACKNOWLEDGMENTS

Because I have been thinking and writing about liberal education for many years, I have more thanks to give than I can properly record here. The many schools, colleges, and universities that have debated the conclusions of my earlier book, *Cultivating Humanity*, must be at the top of the list, as must the Association of American Colleges and Universities, whose members and leaders have been an invaluable source of inspiration and insight. I want to thank Carole Schneider, president of that Association, for involving me in her LEAP report on higher education, and for generously reacting to some of these ideas when I presented them in an earlier form. Mike McPherson of the Spencer Foundation has also been a terrific source of insight, and the year I spent as a resident fellow at the Foundation taught me a lot about this topic, although at the time I was working on a different project. My ongoing association with the Cambridge School in Weston, Massachusetts, where my daughter was educated, gives me optimism about the future of the type of education I defend here. Jane Moulding, the school's head, and all the faculty and trustees are to be honored for their commitment to critical thinking and the arts in an era in which those commitments go against the grain. In a very different way, I get support and nourishment every day from my colleagues at the University of Chicago Law School, an unusual intellectual community where interdisciplinary critical thinking thrives.

One nice feature of working on a topic for many years is that one can trace the ascent of young people one admires to positions of influence. In *Cultivating Humanity*, discussing education for world citizenship, I spoke of a young philosophy professor at St. Lawrence University who pioneered a fine and innovative "intercultural studies" program that involved faculty travel and interdisciplinary teaching. Last April Grant Cornwell became president of the College of Wooster in Ohio, and I was privileged to deliver a lecture based on the ideas in this book at his inauguration.

Most of all, I have been inspired by the education I received as a child, at the Baldwin School in Bryn Mawr, Pennsylvania. I loved being able to go, every day, from a surrounding community focused on profit and success into a space where critical thinking, ideas, and imagination mattered more than profit. I owe the deepest gratitude to my teachers there. I dedicate this book to three of them above all: to Lois Goutman, our inspiring and emotionally probing drama director, who found ways of getting conventional young women to express capacities we did not know we had; to Marthe Melchior, the tiny, fiery professor of French who taught us how to study France from a multidisciplinary perspective, including history, literature, and the arts, and who helped me and my best friend found a French drama club where we even at times wrote our own plays in French, mine a tragedy on the life of Robespierre (at a reunion about ten years ago, then over ninety, but still fiery, she greeted me with, "Vous voyez, Martha, je suis encore jacobine"); and to Marion Stearns, a superb teacher of English poetry and prose, who taught us how to read and write, terrifying us into getting rid of anything false or egotistical in our writing (so difficult for teenage girls to do).

In India I have learned from all my friends in and from Santiniketan, the home of Tagore's school, especially from the late Amita Sen and Amartya Sen. For other conversations about education in India I am grateful to Gurcharan Das, Mushirul Hasan, Zoya Hasan, Pratik Kanjilal, Krishna Kumar, and Antara Dev Sen.

For comments on earlier drafts or pieces of this manuscript, I am grateful to Andrew Koppelman, Mollie Stone, Madhavi Sunder, and my wonderful editor, Rob Tempio.

NOT FOR PROFIT

I

The Silent Crisis

Education is that process by which thought is opened out
of the soul, and, associated with outward things, is reflected
back upon itself, and thus made conscious of their reality
and shape.
                    —Bronson Alcott, Massachusetts educator, c. 1850

[W]hile making use of [material possessions], man has to
be careful to protect himself from [their] tyranny. If he is
weak enough to grow smaller to fit himself to his covering,
then it becomes a process of gradual suicide by shrinkage
of the soul.
                    —Rabindranath Tagore, Indian educator, c. 1917

We are in the midst of a crisis of massive proportions and grave
global significance. No, I do not mean the global economic crisis that began in 2008. At least then everyone knew that a crisis
was at hand, and many world leaders worked quickly and des-
perately to find solutions. Indeed, consequences for governments
were grave if they did not find solutions, and many were replaced
in consequence. No, I mean a crisis that goes largely unnoticed,
like a cancer; a crisis that is likely to be, in the long run, far more

damaging to the future of democratic self-government: a world-wide crisis in education.

Radical changes are occurring in what democratic societies teach the young, and these changes have not been well thought through. Thirsty for national profit, nations, and their systems of education, are heedlessly discarding skills that are needed to keep democracies alive. If this trend continues, nations all over the world will soon be producing generations of useful machines, rather than complete citizens who can think for themselves, criticize tradition, and understand the significance of another person's sufferings and achievements. The future of the world's democracies hangs in the balance.

What are these radical changes? The humanities and the arts are being cut away, in both primary/secondary and college/university education, in virtually every nation of the world. Seen by policy-makers as useless frills, at a time when nations must cut away all useless things in order to stay competitive in the global market, they are rapidly losing their place in curricula, and also in the minds and hearts of parents and children. Indeed, what we might call the humanistic aspects of science and social science—the imaginative, creative aspect, and the aspect of rigorous critical thought—are also losing ground as nations prefer to pursue short-term profit by the cultivation of the useful and highly applied skills suited to profit-making.

This crisis is facing us, but we have not yet faced it. We go on as if everything were business as usual, when in reality great changes of emphasis are evident all over. We haven't really deliberated about these changes, we have not really chosen them, and yet they increasingly limit our future.

Consider these five examples, deliberately drawn from different nations and different educational levels:

- In the fall of 2006 the U.S. Department of Education's Commission on the Future of Higher Education, headed by Bush administration secretary of education Margaret Spellings, released its report on the state of higher education in the nation: *A Test of Leadership: Charting the Future of U.S. Higher Education.*[1] This report contained a valuable critique of unequal access to higher education. When it came to subject matter, however, it focused entirely on education for national economic gain. It concerned itself with perceived deficiencies in science, technology, and engineering—not basic scientific research in these areas, but only highly applied learning, learning that can quickly generate profit-making strategies. The humanities, the arts, and critical thinking were basically absent. By omitting them, the report strongly suggested that it would be perfectly all right if these abilities were allowed to wither away in favor of more useful disciplines.

- In March 2004 a group of scholars from many nations gathered to discuss the educational philosophy of Rabindranath Tagore—winner of the Nobel Prize for Literature in 1913, and leading innovator in education. Tagore's educational experiment, which had wide influence in Europe, Japan, and the United States, focused on the empowerment of the student through practices of Socratic argument, exposure to many world cultures, and, above all, the infusion of music, fine art, theater, and dance into every part of the curriculum. In India today, Tagore's ideas are neglected, and even scorned. Participants in the conference all agreed that a new conception, focused on profit, has taken over—in the process sidelining the whole idea of imaginative and critical self-development through which Tagore had formed so many future citizens of India's successful democracy. Would democracy in India survive today's assault upon its soul? Faced with so much recent evidence of bureaucratic obtuseness and uncritical group-think, many participants feared that the answer might be "No."

- In November 2005 a teachers retreat was held at the Laboratory School in Chicago—the school, on the campus of my own university, where John Dewey conducted his pathbreaking experiments in democratic education reform, the school where President Barack Obama's daughters spent their early formative years. The teachers had gathered to discuss the topic of education for democratic citizenship, and they considered a wide range of educational experiments, studying figures ranging from Socrates to Dewey in the Western tradition to the closely related ideas of Tagore in India. But something was clearly amiss. The teachers—who take pride in stimulating children to question, criticize, and imagine—expressed anxiety about the pressures they face from wealthy parents who send their kids to this elite school. Impatient with allegedly superfluous skills, and intent on getting their children filled with testable skills that seem likely to produce financial success, these parents are trying to change the school's guiding vision. They seem poised to succeed.

- In fall 2005 the head of the search committee for the new dean of the School of Education at one of our nation's most prestigious universities called me for advice. Hereafter I will refer to the university as X. X's School of Education has enormous influence on teachers and schools all over the United States. As I began talking about the role of the humanities and arts in education for democratic citizenship, saying what I took to be familiar and obvious, the woman expressed surprise. "How unusual," she said, "no one else I've talked to has mentioned any of these things at all. We have been talking only about how X University can contribute to scientific and technical education around the world, and that's the thing that our president is really interested in. But what you say is very interesting, and I really want to think about it."

- In the winter of 2006 another prestigious U.S. university— let's call it Y—held a symposium celebrating a major anniversary, a centerpiece of which was to have been discussion of the future of liberal education. A few months before the event, speakers who had agreed to be part of this were told that the focus had been changed and that they should just come and lecture to small departmental audiences on any topic they liked. A helpful and nicely talkative junior administrator told me that the reason for the change was that the president of Y had decided that a symposium on liberal education would not "make a splash," so he decided to replace it with one on the latest achievements in technology and their role in generating profits for business and industry.

There are hundreds of stories like these, and new ones arrive every day, in the United States, in Europe, in India, and, no doubt, in other parts of the world. We are pursuing the possessions that protect, please, and comfort us—what Tagore called our material "covering." But we seem to be forgetting about the soul, about what it is for thought to open out of the soul and connect person to world in a rich, subtle, and complicated manner; about what it is to approach another person as a soul, rather than as a mere useful instrument or an obstacle to one's own plans; about what it is to talk as someone who has a soul to someone else whom one sees as similarly deep and complex.

The word "soul" has religious connotations for many people, and I neither insist on these nor reject them. Each person may hear them or ignore them. What I do insist on, however, is what both Tagore and Alcott meant by this word: the faculties of thought and imagination that make us human and make our relationships rich human relationships, rather than relationships of mere use and manipulation. When we meet in society, if we have not learned to see both self and other in that way, imagining in one another inner faculties of thought and emotion, democracy is bound to fail, because democracy is built upon respect and concern, and these in turn are built upon the ability to see other people as human beings, not simply as objects.

Given that economic growth is so eagerly sought by all nations, especially at this time of crisis, too few questions have been posed about the direction of education, and, with it, of the world's democratic societies. With the rush to profitability in the global market, values precious for the future of democracy, especially in an era of religious and economic anxiety, are in danger of getting lost.

The profit motive suggests to many concerned leaders that science and technology are of crucial importance for the future health of their nations. We should have no objection to good scientific and technical education, and I shall not suggest that nations should stop trying to improve in this regard. My concern is that other abilities, equally crucial, are at risk of getting lost in the competitive flurry, abilities crucial to the health of any democracy internally, and to the creation of a decent world culture capable of constructively addressing the world's most pressing problems.

These abilities are associated with the humanities and the arts: the ability to think critically; the ability to transcend local loyalties and to approach world problems as a "citizen of the world"; and, finally, the ability to imagine sympathetically the predicament of another person.[2]

I shall make my argument by pursuing the contrast that my examples have already suggested: between an education for profit-making and an education for a more inclusive type of citizenship. I shall try to show how the humanities and arts are crucial both in primary/secondary and in university education, drawing examples from a range of different stages and levels. I do not at all deny that science and social science, particularly economics, are also crucial to the education of citizens. But nobody is suggesting leaving these studies behind. I focus, then, on what is both precious and profoundly endangered.

When practiced at their best, moreover, these other disciplines are infused by what we might call the spirit of the humanities: by searching critical thought, daring imagination, empathetic understanding of human experiences of many different kinds, and understanding of the complexity of the world we live in. Science education in recent years has rightly focused on educating the capacities for critical thinking, logical analysis, and imagining. Science, rightly pursued, is a friend of the humanities rather than their enemy. Although good science education is not my theme, a companion study on that topic would be a valuable complement to my focus on the humanities.[3]

The trends I deplore are worldwide, but I shall focus throughout on two very different nations that I know well: the United States, where I live and teach, and India, where my own global development work, much of it focused on education, has been conducted. India has a glorious tradition of humanities and arts education, exemplified in the theory and practice of the great Tagore, and I shall introduce you to his valuable ideas, which laid the foundations for a democratic nation and greatly influenced democratic education in Europe and the United States. But I shall also talk about the role of education in rural literacy projects for women and girls today, where the impetus to empower through the arts remains vital, and the effect of this empowerment on democracy can be clearly seen.

Where the United States is concerned, my argument will range over many types of educational experiments, from the use of Socratic self-examination in schools of many sorts to the role of arts organizations in plugging gaps in the public school curriculum. (The remarkable story of the Chicago Children's Choir in chapter 6 will provide a detailed case study.)

Education does not take place only in schools. Most of the traits that are my focus need to be nurtured in the family as well, both in the early years and as children mature. Part of a comprehensive public policy approach to the questions this manifesto raises must include discussion of how families can be supported in the task of developing children's capabilities. The surrounding peer culture and the larger culture of social norms and political institutions also play an important role, either supporting or subverting the work done by schools and families. The focus on schools, colleges, and universities is justified, however, because it is in these institutions that the most pernicious changes have been taking place, as the pressure for economic growth leads to changes in curriculum, pedagogy, and funding. If we are aware that we are addressing just one part of the story of how citizens develop, we can pursue this focus without distortion.

Education is not just for citizenship. It prepares people for employment and, importantly, for meaningful lives. Another entire book could be written about the role of the arts and humanities in advancing these goals.[4] All modern democracies, however, are societies in which the meaning and ultimate goals of human life are topics of reasonable disagreement among citizens who hold many different religious and secular views, and these citizens will naturally differ about how far various types of humanistic education serve their own particular goals. What we can agree about is that young people all over the world, in any nation lucky enough to be democratic, need to grow up to be participants in a form of government in which the people inform themselves about crucial issues they will address as voters and, sometimes, as elected or appointed officials. Every modern democracy is also a society in which people differ greatly along many parameters, including religion, ethnicity, wealth and class, physical impairment, gender, and sexuality, and in which all voters are making choices that have a major impact on the lives of people who differ from themselves. One way of assessing any educational scheme is to ask how well it prepares young people for life in a form of social and political organization that has these features. Without support from suitably educated citizens, no democracy can remain stable.

I shall argue that cultivated capacities for critical thinking and reflection are crucial in keeping democracies alive and wide awake. The ability to think well about a wide range of cultures, groups, and nations in the context of a grasp of the global economy and of the history of many national and group interactions is crucial in order to enable democracies to deal responsibly with the problems we currently face as members of an interdependent world. And the ability to imagine the experience of another—a capacity almost all human beings possess in some form—needs to be greatly enhanced and refined if we are to have any hope of sustaining decent institutions across the many divisions that any modern society contains.

The national interest of any modern democracy requires a strong economy and a flourishing business culture. As I develop my primary argument, I shall also argue, secondarily, that this economic interest, too, requires us to draw on the humanities and arts, in order to promote a climate of responsible and watchful stewardship and a culture of creative innovation. Thus we are not forced to choose between a form of education that promotes profit and a form of education that promotes good citizenship. A flourishing economy requires the same skills that support citizenship, and thus the proponents of what I shall call "education for profit," or (to put it more comprehensively) "education for economic growth," have adopted an impoverished conception of what is required to meet their own goal. This argument, however, ought to be subservient to the argument concerning the stability of democratic institutions, since a strong economy is a means to human ends, not an end in itself. Most of us would not choose to live in a prosperous nation that had ceased to be democratic. Moreover, although it is clear that a strong business culture requires some people who are imaginative and critical, it is not clear that it requires all people in a nation to gain these skills. Democratic participation makes wider demands, and it is these wider demands that my primary argument supports.

No system of education is doing a good job if its benefits reach only wealthy elites. The distribution of access to quality education is an urgent issue in all modern democracies. The Spellings Commission Report is to be commended for focusing on this question. It has long been a shameful feature of the United States, a wealthy nation, that access to quality primary/secondary education and especially access to college/university education is so unequally distributed. Many developing nations contain even larger disparities in access: India, for example, reports a male literacy rate of only around 65 percent, a female literacy rate of around 50 percent. Urban/rural disparities are larger. In secondary and higher education, there are even more striking gaps—between male and female, between rich and poor, between urban and rural. The lives of children who grow up knowing that they will go on to university and even postgraduate education are utterly different from the lives of children who in many cases do not get a chance to attend school at all. Much good work has been done on this question in many countries. It is not, however, the topic of this book.

This book is about what we should be striving for. Until we are clear about this, it is difficult to figure out how to get it to those who need it.

II

Education for Profit, Education for Democracy

We, the People of the United States, in Order to form a more perfect Union, establish Justice, insure domestic Tranquility, provide for the common defence, promote the general Welfare, and secure the Blessings of Liberty to ourselves and our Posterity, do ordain and establish this Constitution for the United States of America.

—Preamble, *Constitution of the United States,* 1787

WE, THE PEOPLE OF INDIA, having solemnly resolved to . . . secure to all its citizens:
JUSTICE, economic and political;
LIBERTY of thought, expression, belief, faith and worship;
EQUALITY of status and of opportunity
and to promote among them all
FRATERNITY assuring the dignity of the individual and the unity and integrity of the Nation;
IN OUR CONSTITUENT ASSEMBLY this twenty-sixth day of November, 1949, do HEREBY ADOPT, ENACT AND GIVE TO OURSELVES THIS CONSTITUTION.

—Preamble, *Constitution of India,* 1949

Education shall be directed to the full development of the
human personality and to the strengthening of respect for
human rights and fundamental freedoms. It shall promote
understanding, tolerance and friendship among all nations,
racial or religious groups.
—*Universal Declaration of Human Rights,* 1948

To think about education for democratic citizenship, we have to
think about what democratic nations are, and what they strive for.
What does it mean, then, for a nation to advance? In one view it
means to increase its gross national product per capita. This measure of national achievement has for decades been the standard
one used by development economists around the world, as if it
were a good proxy for a nation's overall quality of life.

The goal of a nation, says this model of development, should
be economic growth. Never mind about distribution and social
equality, never mind about the preconditions of stable democracy,
never mind about the quality of race and gender relations, never
mind about the improvement of other aspects of a human being's
quality of life that are not well linked to economic growth. (Empirical studies have by now shown that political liberty, health,
and education are all poorly correlated with growth.)[1] One sign
of what this model leaves out is the fact that South Africa under apartheid used to shoot to the top of development indices.
There was a lot of wealth in the old South Africa, and the old
model of development rewarded that achievement (or good for-
tune), ignoring the staggering distributional inequalities, the bru-
tal apartheid regime, and the health and educational deficiencies
that went with it.

This model of development has by now been rejected by many

serious development thinkers, but it continues to dominate a lot of policy-making, especially policies influenced by the United States. The World Bank made some commendable progress, under James Wolfensohn, in recognizing a richer conception of development, but things then slipped badly, and the International Monetary Fund never made the sort of progress that the Bank did under Wolfensohn. Many nations, and states within nations, are pursuing this model of development. Today's India offers a revealing laboratory of such experiments, as some states (Gujarat, Andhra Pradesh) have pursued economic growth through foreign investment, doing little for health, education, and the condition of the rural poor, while other states (Kerala, Delhi, to some extent West Bengal) have pursued more egalitarian strategies, trying to ensure that health and education are available to all, that the infrastructure develops in a way that serves all, and that investment is tied to job creation for the poorest.

Proponents of the old model sometimes like to claim that the pursuit of economic growth will by itself deliver the other good things I have mentioned: health, education, a decrease in social and economic inequality. By now, however, examining the results of these divergent experiments, we have discovered that the old model really does not deliver the goods as claimed. Achievements in health and education, for example, are very poorly correlated with economic growth.[2] Nor does political liberty track growth, as we can see from the stunning success of China. So producing economic growth does not mean producing democracy. Nor does it mean producing a healthy, engaged, educated population in which opportunities for a good life are available to all social classes. Still, everyone likes economic growth these days, and the trend is, if anything, toward increasing reliance on what I have called the "old paradigm," rather than toward a more complex account of what societies should be trying to achieve for their people.

These baneful trends have recently been challenged in both of the nations that are my focus. By choosing the Obama administration, U.S. voters opted for a group committed to greater equality in health care and a greater degree of attention to issues of equal access to opportunity generally. In India, this past May, in a surprise result, voters delivered a virtual majority to the Congress party, which has combined moderate economic reforms with a strong commitment to the rural poor.[3] In neither nation, however, have policies been sufficiently rethought with ideas of human development clearly in view. Thus it is not clear that either nation has really embraced a human development paradigm, as opposed to a growth-oriented paradigm adjusted for distribution.

Both nations, however, have written constitutions, and in both, the constitution protects from majority whim a group of fundamental rights that cannot be abrogated even to achieve a large economic benefit. Both nations protect a range of political and civil rights, and both guarantee all citizens the equal protection of the laws regardless of racial, gender, or religious group membership. The Indian list, longer than that of the United States, also includes free compulsory primary and secondary education, and a right to freedom from desperate conditions (a life commensurate with human dignity).[4] Even though the U.S. federal Constitution does not guarantee a right to education, numerous state constitutions do, and many add other social welfare provisions. In general, we are entitled to conclude that both the United States and India have rejected the notion that the right way for a nation to proceed is simply to strive to maximize economic growth. It is, then, all the odder that major figures concerned with education, in both nations, continue to behave as if the goal of education were economic growth alone.

In the context of the old paradigm of what it is for a nation to develop, what is on everyone's lips is the need for an education that promotes national development seen as economic growth. Such an education has recently been outlined by the Spellings Commission Report of the U.S. Department of Education, focusing on higher education. It is being implemented by many European nations, as they give high marks to technical universities and university departments and impose increasingly draconian cuts on the humanities. It is central to discussions of education in India today, as in most developing nations that are trying to grab a larger share of the global market.

The United States has never had a pure growth-directed model of education. Some distinctive and by now traditional features of our system positively resist being cast in those terms. Unlike virtually every nation in the world, we have a liberal arts model of university education. Instead of entering college/university to study a single subject, students are required to take a wide range of courses in their first two years, prominently including courses in the humanities. This model of university and college education influences secondary education. Nobody is tracked too early into a nonhumanities stream, whether purely scientific or purely vocational, nor do children with a humanities focus lose all contact with the sciences at an early date. Nor is the emphasis on the liberal arts a vestige of elitism or class distinction. From early on, leading U.S. educators connected the liberal arts to the preparation of informed, independent, and sympathetic democratic citizens. The liberal arts model is still relatively strong, but it is under severe stress now in this time of economic hardship.

Another aspect of the U.S. educational tradition that stubbornly refuses assimilation into the growth-directed model is its characteristic emphasis on the active participation of the child in inquiry and questioning. This model of learning, associated with a long Western philosophical tradition of education theory, ranging from Jean-Jacques Rousseau in the eighteenth century to John Dewey in the twentieth, includes such eminent educators as Friedrich Froebel in Germany, Johann Pestalozzi in Switzerland, Bronson Alcott in the United States, and Maria Montessori in Italy. In chapter 4 we shall discuss their ideas further. This tradition argues that education is not just about the passive assimilation of facts and cultural traditions, but about challenging the mind to become active, competent, and thoughtfully critical in a complex world. This model of education supplanted an older one in which children sat still at desks all day and simply absorbed, and then regurgitated, the material that was brought their way. This idea of active learning, which usually includes a large commitment to critical thinking and argument that traces its roots back to Socrates, has profoundly influenced American primary and to some extent secondary education, and this influence has not yet ceased, despite increasing pressures on schools to produce the sort of student who can do well on a standardized test.

I shall discuss these educational theories later, but I introduce them now in order to point out that we are unlikely to find a pure example of education for economic growth in the United States—*so far.* India is closer; for, despite the widespread influence of the great Tagore, who tried to build his school around the idea of critical thinking and empathetic imagining, and who founded a university built around an interdisciplinary liberal arts model, India's universities today, like those of Europe, have long been structured around the single-subject rather than the liberal arts paradigm. Tagore's university, Visva-Bharati (which means "All-the-World"), was taken over by the government, and now it is just like any other single-subject-model university, largely aiming at market impact. Similarly, Tagore's school has long ceased to define the goals of primary and secondary education. Socratic active learning and exploration through the arts have been rejected in favor of a pedagogy of force-feeding for standardized national examinations. The very model of learning that Tagore (along with the Europeans and Americans I have named) passionately repudiated—in which the student sits passively at a desk while teachers and textbooks present material to be uncritically assimilated—is a ubiquitous reality in India's government schools. When we imagine what education for economic growth would be like, pursued without attention to other goals, we are likely, then, to come up with something that lies relatively close to what India's government-sector schools usually offer.

Nonetheless, our aim is to understand a model that has influence around the world, not to describe a particular school system in a particular nation, so let us simply pose our questions abstractly.

What sort of education does the old model of development suggest? Education for economic growth needs basic skills, literacy, and numeracy. It also needs some people to have more advanced skills in computer science and technology. Equal access, however, is not terribly important; a nation can grow very nicely while the rural poor remain illiterate and without basic computer resources, as recent events in many Indian states show. In states such as Gujarat and Andhra Pradesh, we have seen the creation of increased GNP per capita through the education of a technical elite who make the state attractive to foreign investors. The results of this growth have not trickled down to improve the health and well-being of the rural poor, and there is no reason to think that economic growth requires educating them adequately. This was always the first and most basic problem with the GNP per capita paradigm of development. It neglects distribution, and can give high marks to nations or states that contain alarming inequalities. This is very true of education: Given the nature of the information economy, nations can increase their GNP without worrying too much about the distribution of education, so long as they create a competent technology and business elite.

Here we see yet another way in which the United States has traditionally diverged, at least in theory, from the economic growth paradigm. In the U.S. tradition of public education, ideas of equal opportunity and equal access, though never robust in reality, have always been notional goals, defended even by the most growth-focused politicians, such as the authors of the Spellings Report.

After basic skills for many, and more advanced skills for some, education for economic growth needs a very rudimentary familiarity with history and with economic fact—on the part of the people who are going to get past elementary education in the first place, and who may turn out to be a relatively small elite. But care must be taken lest the historical and economic narrative lead to any serious critical thinking about class, about race and gender, about whether foreign investment is really good for the rural poor, about whether democracy can survive when huge inequalities in basic life-chances obtain. So critical thinking would not be a very important part of education for economic growth, and it has not been in states that have pursued this goal relentlessly, such as the Western Indian state of Gujarat, well known for its combination of technological sophistication with docility and group-think. The student's freedom of mind is dangerous if what is wanted is a group of technically trained obedient workers to carry out the plans of elites who are aiming at foreign investment and technological development. Critical thinking will, then, be discouraged—as it has so long been in the government schools of Gujarat.

History, I said, might be essential. But educators for economic growth will not want a study of history that focuses on injustices of class, caste, gender, and ethnoreligious membership, because this will prompt critical thinking about the present. Nor will such educators want any serious consideration of the rise of nationalism, of the damages done by nationalist ideals, and of the way in which the moral imagination too often becomes numbed under the sway of technical mastery—all themes developed with scathing pessimism by Rabindranath Tagore in *Nationalism*, lectures delivered during the First World War, which are ignored in today's India, despite the universal fame of Tagore as Nobel Prize–winning author.[5] So the version of history that will be presented will present national ambition, especially ambition for wealth, as a great good, and will downplay issues of poverty and of global accountability. Once again, real-life examples of this sort of education are easy to find.

A salient example of this approach to history can be found in the textbooks created by the BJP, India's Hindu-nationalist political party, which also pursues aggressively an economic-growth-based development agenda. These books (now, fortunately, withdrawn, since the BJP lost power in 2004) utterly discouraged critical thinking and didn't even give it material to work with. They presented India's history as an uncritical story of material and cultural triumph in which all trouble was caused by outsiders and internal "foreign elements." Criticism of injustices in India's past was made virtually impossible by the content of the material and by its suggested pedagogy (for example, the questions at the end of each chapter), which discouraged thoughtful questioning and urged assimilation and regurgitation. Students were asked simply to absorb a story of unblemished goodness, bypassing all inequalities of caste, gender, and religion.

Contemporary development issues, too, were presented with an emphasis on the paramount importance of economic growth and the relative insignificance of distributional equality. Students were told that what matters is the situation of the *average* person (not, for example, how the least well-off are doing). And they were even encouraged to think of themselves as parts of a large collectivity that is making progress, rather than as separate people with separate entitlements: "In social development, whatever benefit an individual derives is only as a collective being."[6] This controversial norm (which suggests that if the nation is doing well, you must be doing well, even if you are extremely poor and suffering from many deprivations) is presented as a fact that students must memorize and regurgitate on mandatory national examinations.

Education for economic growth is likely to have such features everywhere, since the unfettered pursuit of growth is not conducive to sensitive thinking about distribution or social inequality. (Inequality can reach astonishing proportions, as it did in yesterday's South Africa, while a nation grows very nicely.) Indeed, putting a human face on poverty is likely to produce hesitation about the pursuit of growth; for foreign investment often needs to be courted by policies that strongly disadvantage the rural poor. (In many parts of India, for example, poor agricultural laborers hold down land that is needed to build factories, and they are not likely to be the gainers when their land is acquired by the government— even if they are compensated, they do not typically have the skills to be employed in the new industries that displace them.)[7]

What about the arts and literature, so often valued by democratic educators? An education for economic growth will, first of all, have contempt for these parts of a child's training, because they don't look like they lead to personal or national economic advancement. For this reason, all over the world, programs in arts and the humanities, at all levels, are being cut away, in favor of the cultivation of the technical. Indian parents take pride in a child who gains admission to the Institutes of Technology and Management; they are ashamed of a child who studies literature, or philosophy, or who wants to paint or dance or sing. American parents, too, are moving rapidly in this direction, despite a long liberal arts tradition.

But educators for economic growth will do more than ignore the arts. They will fear them. For a cultivated and developed sympathy is a particularly dangerous enemy of obtuseness, and moral obtuseness is necessary to carry out programs of economic development that ignore inequality. It is easier to treat people as objects to be manipulated if you have never learned any other way to see them. As Tagore said, aggressive nationalism needs to blunt the moral conscience, so it needs people who do not recognize the individual, who speak group-speak, who behave, and see the world, like docile bureaucrats. Art is a great enemy of that obtuseness, and artists (unless thoroughly browbeaten and corrupted) are not the reliable servants of any ideology, even a basically good one—they always ask the imagination to move beyond its usual confines, to see the world in new ways.[8] So, educators for economic growth will campaign against the humanities and arts as ingredients of basic education. This assault is currently taking place all over the world.

Pure models of education for economic growth are difficult to find in flourishing democracies since democracy is built on respect for each person, and the growth model respects only an aggregate. However, education systems all over the world are moving closer and closer to the growth model without much thought about how ill-suited it is to the goals of democracy.

How else might we think of the sort of nation and the sort of citizen we are trying to build? The primary alternative to the growth-based model in international development circles, and one with which I have been associated, is known as the Human Development paradigm. According to this model, what is important is the opportunities, or "capabilities," each person has in key areas ranging from life, health, and bodily integrity to political liberty, political participation, and education. This model of development recognizes that all individuals possess an inalienable human dignity that must be respected by laws and institutions. A decent nation, at a bare minimum, acknowledges that its citizens have entitlements in these and other areas and devises strategies to get people above a threshold level of opportunity in each.

The Human Development model is committed to democracy, since having a voice in the choice of the policies that govern one's life is a key ingredient of a life worthy of human dignity. The sort of democracy it favors will, however, be one with a strong role for fundamental rights that cannot be taken away from people by majority whim—it will thus favor strong protections for political liberty; the freedoms of speech, association, and religious exercise; and fundamental entitlements in yet other areas such as education and health. This model dovetails well with the aspirations pursued in India's constitution (and that of South Africa). The United States has never given constitutional protection, at least at the federal level, to entitlements in "social and economic" areas such as health and education; and yet Americans, too, have a strong sense that the ability of all citizens to attain these entitlements is an important mark of national success. So the Human Development model is not pie-in-the-sky idealism; it is closely related to the constitutional commitments, not always completely fulfilled, of many if not most of the world's democratic nations.

If a nation wants to promote this type of humane, people-sensitive democracy dedicated to promoting opportunities for "life, liberty and the pursuit of happiness" to each and every person, what abilities will it need to produce in its citizens? At least the following seem crucial:

- The ability to think well about political issues affecting the nation, to examine, reflect, argue, and debate, deferring to neither tradition nor authority

- The ability to recognize fellow citizens as people with equal rights, even though they may be different in race, religion, gender, and sexuality: to look at them with respect, as ends, not just as tools to be manipulated for one's own profit

- The ability to have concern for the lives of others, to grasp what policies of many types mean for the opportunities and experiences of one's fellow citizens, of many types, and for people outside one's own nation

- The ability to imagine well a variety of complex issues affecting the story of a human life as it unfolds: to think about childhood, adolescence, family relationships, illness, death, and much more in a way informed by an understanding of a wide range of human stories, not just by aggregate data

- The ability to judge political leaders critically, but with an informed and realistic sense of the possibilities available to them

- The ability to think about the good of the nation as a whole, not just that of one's own local group

- The ability to see one's own nation, in turn, as a part of a complicated world order in which issues of many kinds require intelligent transnational deliberation for their resolution

This is only a sketch, but it is at least a beginning in articulating what we need.

III

Educating Citizens: The Moral (and Anti-Moral) Emotions

A child's first sentiment is to love himself; and the second, which derives from the first, is to love those who come near him, for in the state of weakness that he is in, he does not recognize anyone except by the assistance and care he receives.
—Jean-Jacques Rousseau, *Emile: or, On Education*, Book IV, 1762

If democracy is maturity, and maturity is health, and health is desirable, then we wish to see whether anything can be done to foster it.
—Donald Winnicott, "Thoughts on the Meaning of the Word Democracy," 1950

Education is for people. Before we can design a scheme for education, we need to understand the problems we face on the way to making students responsible democratic citizens who might think and choose well about a wide range of issues of national and worldwide significance. What is it about human life that makes it so hard to sustain democratic institutions based on equal respect and the equal protection of the laws, and so easy to lapse into hierarchies of various types—or, even worse, projects of violent group animosity? What forces make powerful groups seek control and domination? What makes majorities try, so ubiquitously, to denigrate or stigmatize minorities? Whatever these forces are, it is ultimately against them that true education for responsible national and global citizenship must fight. And it must fight using whatever resources the human personality contains that help democracy prevail against hierarchy.

We Americans are sometimes told that evil is something that exists for the most part outside of us. Witness the rhetorical construction of an "axis of evil" that threatens our own good nation. People find it comforting to see themselves as engaged in a titanic "clash of civilizations" in which good democratic nations are pitted against allegedly bad religions and cultures from other parts of the world. Popular culture all too often feeds this way of seeing the world, by portraying the good characters' problems as ended by the death of some "bad guys." Non-Western cultures are not immune from these pernicious ways of thinking. The Hindu Right in India, for example, has long portrayed India as locked in a struggle between the good and pure forces of Hinduism and a set of dangerous "foreign elements" (by which they mean Muslims and Christians, although both groups are no less indigenous to the subcontinent than are Hindus).[1] In the process they have enlisted popular culture, retelling classical epic tales, in popular televised versions, in a way that removes all complexity in their depiction of "good" and "bad" characters and that encourages viewers to identify the "bad" characters with a contemporary Muslim threat.[2]

Such myths of purity, however, are misleading and pernicious. No society is pure, and the "clash of civilizations" is internal to every society. Every society contains within itself people who are prepared to live with others on terms of mutual respect and reciprocity, and people who seek the comfort of domination. We need to understand how to produce more citizens of the former sort and fewer of the latter. Thinking falsely that our own society is pure within can only breed aggression toward outsiders and blindness about aggression toward insiders.

How do people become capable of respect and democratic equality? What makes them seek domination? To answer such questions, we must pursue the "clash of civilizations" at a deeper level, understanding the forces within each and every person that militate against mutual respect and reciprocity, as well as the forces that give democracy strong support. One of our world's most creative democratic political leaders, Mahatma Gandhi, one of the primary architects of an independent and democratic India, understood very well that the political struggle for freedom and equality must first of all be a struggle within each person, as compassion and respect contend against fear, greed, and narcissistic aggression. He repeatedly drew attention to the connection between psychological balance and political balance, arguing that greedy desire, aggression, and narcissistic anxiety are forces inimical to the building of a free and democratic nation.

The internal clash of civilizations can be observed in many struggles over inclusion and equality that take place in modern societies: debates about immigration; about the accommodation of religious, racial, and ethnic minorities; about gender equality; about sexual orientation; about affirmative action. In all societies, these debates give rise to anxiety and aggression. In all, too, there are forces of compassion and respect. Particular social and political structures make a big difference to the outcome of these struggles, but we would do well to work, at least tentatively, with a widely shared narrative of human childhood, in order to locate within it problems and resources that both institutions and social norms can further develop or inhibit.[3] Pinning down the details of any such account is a matter for ongoing research and argument; investigating possible intervention points is equally complex. But we have to begin somewhere, and many proposals for education do not spell out a psychology of human development at all, so it remains unclear what problems need to be solved, or what resources we have for solving them.

Human infants are born, helpless, into a world that they did not make and do not control. An infant's earliest experiences contain a jolting alternation between blissful completeness, in which the whole world seems to revolve around the satisfaction of its needs— as in the womb—and an agonizing awareness of helplessness, when good things do not arrive at the desired moment, and the infant can do nothing to ensure their arrival. Human beings have a level of physical helplessness unknown elsewhere in the animal kingdom—combined with a very high level of cognitive sophistication. (We know now, for example, that even a baby one week old can tell the difference between the smell of its own mother's milk and milk from another mother.) Understanding what the "clash within" is all about requires thinking about this strange sui generis narrative: about human beings' strange combination of competence with helplessness; our problematic relationship to helplessness, mortality, and finitude; our persistent desire to transcend conditions that are painful for any intelligent being to accept.

As infants develop, they are increasingly aware of what is happening to them, but they cannot do anything about it. The expectation of being attended to constantly—the "infantile omnipotence" so well captured in Freud's phrase "His Majesty the baby"—is joined to the anxiety, and the shame, of knowing that one is not in fact omnipotent, but completely powerless. Out of this anxiety and shame emerges an urgent desire for completeness and fullness that never completely departs, however much children learn that they are but one part of a world of finite needy beings. And this desire to transcend the shame of incompleteness leads to much instability and moral danger.

To infants at this early point, other people are not fully real; they are just instruments that either bring what is needed or do not. Infants would really like to make their parents their slaves in order to control the forces that supply what they need. Jean-Jacques Rousseau, in his great work on education, *Emile*, saw in children's desire to enslave their parents the beginning of a world of hierarchy. Though Rousseau did not think children evil by nature—indeed he emphasized their natural instincts toward love and compassion—he understood that the very weakness and neediness of human infants gives rise to a dynamic that can create ethical deformation and cruel behavior, unless narcissism and the tendency to dominate are channeled in a more productive direction.

I have mentioned children's shame at their helplessness—their inability to achieve the blissful completeness that at certain moments they are led to expect.[4] This shame, which we may call "primitive shame," is soon joined to another very powerful emotion: disgust at one's own bodily waste products. Disgust, like most emotions, has an innate evolutionary basis, but it also involves learning, and it does not appear until the time of toilet training, when the child's cognitive capacities are quite mature. Society, therefore, has a lot of room to influence the direction it takes. Recent research on disgust shows that it is not merely visceral; it has a strong cognitive component, involving ideas of contamination or defilement. In disgust, experimental psychologists have concluded, we reject as contaminating those things—feces, other bodily waste products, and the corpse—that are the evidence of our own animality and mortality, and thus of our helplessness in important matters. Experimental psychologists working on disgust agree that in distancing ourselves from these waste products we are managing our anxiety about having, and ultimately being, waste products, and thus animal and mortal, ourselves.[5]

So described, disgust looks like it might give us good guidance, since the aversion to feces and corpses probably has utility, as a rough heuristic for the avoidance of danger. Although disgust tracks the sense of danger very imperfectly—many dangerous substances in nature are not disgusting, and many disgusting things are harmless—avoiding milk that smells disgusting is sensible, and easier than testing it in the lab each time.[6] Disgust soon begins to do real damage, however, in connection with the basic narcissism of human children. One effective way to distance oneself thoroughly from one's own animality is to project the properties of animality—bad smell, ooziness, sliminess—onto some group of people, and then to treat those people as contaminating or defiling, turning them into an underclass, and, in effect, a boundary, or a buffer zone, between the anxious person and the feared and stigmatized properties of animality. Children begin to do this very early, identifying some children as dirty or defiling. One example of this is the common child's game of making a folded paper device called a "cootie catcher," and using it, in play, to "catch" allegedly disgusting bugs, or "cooties," off of unpopular children who are stigmatized as dirty and disgusting.

Meanwhile, children learn from the adult societies around them, which typically direct this "projective disgust" onto one or more concrete subordinate groups—African Americans, Jews, women, homosexuals, poor people, lower castes in the Indian caste hierarchy. In effect, these groups function as the animal "other" by the exclusion of which a privileged group defines itself as superior, even transcendent. A common manifestation of projective disgust is to avoid bodily contact with members of the subordinate group, and even to avoid contact with objects that members of this group have touched. Disgust, as psychological research emphasizes, is full of irrational magical thinking. It is no surprise that ideas of contamination are ubiquitous in racism and other types of group subordination.

Projective disgust is always a suspect emotion, because it involves self-repudiation and the displacement of self-repudiation onto another group that is really just a set of bodily human beings like the ones doing the projecting, only more socially powerless. In this way, the narcissistic child's original desire to turn parents into slaves finds fulfillment—by the creation of a social hierarchy. This dynamic is a constant threat to democratic equality.[7]

This story appears to be universal in some form: studies of disgust in many societies reveal similar dynamics, and we must acknowledge, sadly, that all human societies have created out-groups who are stigmatized as either shameful or disgusting, and usually both. Nonetheless, there are numerous sources of variation that affect the outcome of this story, by shaping people's attitudes toward weakness, need, and interdependence. These include individual family differences, social norms, and law. Typically these three interact with one another in complex ways, since parents are themselves inhabitants of a social and political world, and the signals they send to their children are shaped by that world.

Because stigmatizing behavior seems to be a reaction to anxiety about one's own weakness and vulnerability, it cannot be moderated without addressing that deeper anxiety. One part of addressing it that Rousseau emphasized is learning practical competence. Children who can negotiate well in their environment have less need for servants to wait on them. But another part of the social response has to be directed at the sense of helplessness itself, and the pain it causes. Some social and familial norms creatively address this pain, sending a message to young people that human beings are all vulnerable and mortal, and that this aspect of human life is not to be hated and repudiated, but addressed by reciprocity and mutual aid. Jean-Jacques Rousseau made the learning of basic human weakness central to his whole scheme for education, saying that only cognizance of that weakness makes us sociable and turns us to humanity; thus our very inadequacy can become the basis of our hope of a decent community. He pointed out that the nobles of France did not have such an education; they grew up learning that they were above the common lot of human life. This desire for invulnerability fueled their desire to lord it over others.

Many societies teach the bad lessons that Rousseau's French nobles learned. Through both social and familial norms, they send the message that perfection, invulnerability, and control are key aspects of adult success. In many cultures, such social norms take a gendered form, and the disgust research has found that there is frequently a strong gendered component to the projection of disgustingness onto others. Males learn that success means being above the body and its frailties, so they learn to characterize some underclass (women, African Americans) as hyperbodily, thus in need of being dominated. This story has many cultural variations, which need to be studied closely before they can be addressed in a particular society. Even when a culture as a whole does not contain such diseased norms, individual families may still send bad messages, for example that the only way to succeed is to be perfect and to control everything. So the sources of social hierarchy lie deep in human life; the "internal clash" can never be fought on the terrain of the school or university alone, but must involve the family and the larger society. Schools, however, are at least one influential force in a child's life, and one whose messages we are likely to be able to monitor more easily than others.

A central part of disgust's pathology, we said, is the bifurcation of the world into the "pure" and the "impure"—the construction of a "we" who are without flaw and a "they" who are dirty, evil, and contaminating. Much bad thinking about international politics shows the traces of this pathology, as people prove all too ready to think about some group of others as black and sullied, while they themselves are on the side of the angels. We now notice that this very deep-seated human tendency is nourished by many time-honored modes of storytelling to children, which suggest that the world will be set right when some ugly and disgusting witch or monster is killed, or even cooked in her own oven.[8] Many contemporary stories for children purvey the same worldview. We should be grateful for artists who suggest to children the world's real complexity: the Japanese filmmaker Hayao

Miyazaki, for example, whose wild and fantastic films contain a view of good and evil that is both gentler and more nuanced, in which dangers may come from such real and complex sources as decent humans' relation to the environment; or Maurice Sendak, whose Max, in *Where the Wild Things Are*—which has now become an impressive film—romps with monsters that represent his own inner world and the dangerous aggression that lurks there. Nor are the monsters even entirely hideous; for the hatred of one's own internal demons is a frequent source of the need to project them outward onto others. Stories learned in childhood become powerful constituents of the world we inhabit as adults.

I have spoken of problems; what of resources? The other side of the internal clash is the child's growing capacity for compassionate concern, for seeing another person as an end and not a mere means. As time goes on, if all goes well, children come to feel gratitude and love toward the separate beings who support their needs, and they become increasingly able to imagine the world from these people's point of view. This ability to feel concern and to respond with sympathy and imaginative perspective is a deep part of our evolutionary heritage.[9] Primates of many sorts seem to experience some type of sympathy, as do elephants, and probably dogs. In the case of chimpanzees and probably dogs and elephants, sympathy is combined with empathy, that is, a capacity for "positional thinking," the ability to see the world from another creature's viewpoint. Positional thinking is not necessary for sympathy, and it is surely not sufficient; a sadist may use it to torture a victim. It is, however, a great help toward forming sympathetic emotions—which, in turn, are correlated with helping behavor. The striking experimental work of C. Daniel Batson shows that people who are asked to attend to a vivid narrative of someone else's plight, taking up the other person's point of view, are far more apt to respond sympathetically than people who are asked to listen in a more distanced way. Having responded with sympathetic emotion, they then choose to help the other person—if there is an option presented to them, not too costly, that makes such help possible.[10]

Children who develop a capacity for sympathy or compassion—often through empathetic perspectival experience—understand what their aggression has done to another separate person, for whom they increasingly care. They thus come to feel guilt about their own aggression and real concern for the well-being of the other person. Empathy is not morality, but it can supply crucial ingredients of morality. As concern develops, it leads to an increasing wish to control one's own aggression; children recognize that other people are not their slaves but separate beings with the right to lives of their own.

Such recognitions are typically unstable, since human life is a chancy business and we all feel anxieties that lead us to want more control, including control over other people. But a positive upbringing in the family, coupled with a good education later, can make children feel compassionate concern for the needs of others, and can lead them to see others as people with rights equal to their own. To the extent that social norms and dominant social images of adulthood or masculinity interfere with that formation, there will be difficulty and tension, but a good education can combat such stereotypes, giving children a sense of the importance of empathy and reciprocity.

Compassion is not reliable in and of itself. Like the other animals, human beings typically feel compassion toward those they know, and not toward those they don't know. We now know that even creatures as apparently simple as mice respond with discomfort to the bodily discomfort of other mice—*if* they have previously lived with those particular mice.[11] The pain of mice who are strangers, however, fails to produce the emotional contagion that is a precursor of sympathy. So the tendency to segment the world into the known and the unknown probably lies very deep in our evolutionary heritage.

We may also withhold compassion for other bad reasons; for example, we might wrongly blame the suffering person for her misfortune. Many Americans think that poor people bring poverty on themselves through laziness and lack of effort. Consequently, though often wrong about this, they do not feel compassion for poor people.[12]

These deficiencies in compassion can hook up with the pernicious dynamic of disgust and shame. When a particular subgroup in society has been identified as shameful and disgusting, its members seem beneath the dominant ones, and very different from them: animal, smelly, contaminated, and contaminating. So it becomes easy to exclude them from compassion, and hard to see the world from their point of view. White people who feel great compassion for other white people can treat people of color like animals or objects, refusing to see the world from their perspective. Men often treat women this way, while feeling sympathy for other men. In short, cultivating compassion is not, all by itself, sufficient to overcome the forces of enslavement and subordination, since compassion itself can become an ally of disgust and shame, strengthening solidarity among elites and distancing them yet further from the subordinated.

As young people near adulthood, the influence of the surrounding peer culture increases. Norms of the good adult (the good man, the good woman) make a great impact on the developmental process, as concern contends against narcissistic insecurity and shame. If an adolescent peer culture defines the "real man" as one who has no weakness or need, and who controls everything that he requires in life, such a teaching will feed infantile narcissism and strongly inhibit the extension of compassion to women and other people perceived as weak or subordinate. Psychologists Dan Kindlon and Michael Thompson observed such a culture operating among teenage boys in America.[13] To some degree all cultures portray manliness as involving control, but certainly American culture does, as it holds up to the young the image of the lone cowboy who can provide for himself without any help.

As Kindlon and Thompson stress, the attempt to be that ideal man involves a pretense of control in a world that one does not really control. This pretense is unmasked virtually every day by life itself, as the young "real man" feels hunger, fatigue, longing, often illness or fear. So an undercurrent of shame runs through the psyche of any person who lives by this myth; I am supposed to be a "real man," but I feel that I do not control my own surroundings, or even my own body in countless ways. If shame is a virtually universal response to human helplessness, it is far more intense in people who have been brought up on the myth of total control, rather than on an ideal of mutual need and interdependency. Once again, then, we can see how crucial it is for children not to aspire to control or invulnerability, defining their prospects and possibilities as above the common lot of human life, but, instead, to learn to appreciate vividly the ways in which common human weaknesses are experienced in a wide range of social circumstances, understanding how social and political arrangements of different kinds affect the vulnerabilities that all human beings share.

Rousseau argues that the educator must combat Emile's narcissistic desire to lord it over others from two directions. On the one hand, as he becomes physically mature, he must learn not to be helpless, not to need to be waited on hand and foot. To the extent that he is competent in the world, he will have less need to call on others the way a baby does, and he can less anxiously view them as people with projects of their own, who are not at his beck and call. Most schools, Rousseau thought, encourage helplessness and passivity by presenting learning purely abstractly, in a way that is detached from any practical employment. His educator, by contrast, would teach Emile to negotiate in the world he inhabits, making him a competent participant in that world's activities. On the other hand, Emile's emotional education must continue; through a wide range of narratives, he must learn to identify with the lot of others, to see the world through their eyes, and to feel their sufferings vividly through the imagination. Only in that way will other people, at a distance, become real and equal to him.

This story of narcissism, helplessness, shame, disgust, and compassion lies, I believe, at the heart of what education for democratic citizenship must address. But there are other psychological issues that the educator will need to keep in mind. Research in experimental psychology has revealed a number of pernicious tendencies that seem to be common to a wide range of societies. Stanley Milgram, in his well-known and by now classic experiments, demonstrated that experimental subjects have a high level of deference to authority. Most people in his often-repeated experiments were willing to administer a very painful and dangerous level of electric shock to another person, so long as the superintending scientist told them that what they were doing was all right—even when the other person was screaming in pain (which, of course, was faked for the sake of the experiment).[14] Solomon Asch, earlier, showed that experimental subjects are willing to go against the clear evidence of their senses when all the other people around them are making sensory judgments that are off-target; his rigorous and oft-confirmed research shows the unusual subservience of normal human beings to peer pressure. Both Milgram's work and Asch's have been used effectively by Christopher Browning to illuminate the behavior of young Germans in a police battalion that murdered Jews during the Nazi era.[15] So great was the influence of both peer pressure and authority on these young men, Browning shows, that the ones who couldn't bring themselves to shoot Jews felt ashamed of their weakness.

It is easy to see that these two tendencies lie close to the narcissism/insecurity/shame dynamic I described above. People like solidarity with a peer group because it is a type of surrogate invulnerability, and it is no surprise that when people stigmatize and persecute others, they do so, often, as members of a solidaristic group. Subservience to authority is a common feature of group life, and trust in a leader whom one sees as invulnerable is a well-known way in which the fragile ego protects itself against insecurity. In one sense, then, this research confirms the narrative I have just mapped out.

The research, however, tells us something new. It shows that people who have roughly similar underlying tendencies behave worse if their situation has been designed in a particular way. The Asch research showed that if even one dissenter was present, the subject was able to voice his or her own independent judgment; being utterly surrounded with people who made the mistaken judgment was what stopped the subject from saying what she thought. The Milgram research shows that allowing people to think that they are not responsible for their own decisions, because an authority figure has taken responsibility, produces irresponsible decisions. In short, the same people who might behave well in a situation of a different type behave badly in specific structures.

Still other research demonstrates that apparently decent and well-behaved people are willing to engage in behavior that humiliates and stigmatizes if their situation is set up in a certain way, casting them in a dominant role and telling them that the others are their inferiors. One particularly chilling example involves schoolchildren whose teacher informs them that children with blue eyes are superior to children with dark eyes. Hierarchical and cruel behavior ensues. The teacher then informs the children that a mistake has been made; it is actually the brown-eyed children who are superior, the blue-eyed inferior. The hierarchical and cruel behavior simply reverses itself; the brown-eyed children seem to have learned nothing from the pain of discrimination.[16] In short, bad behavior is not just the result of a diseased individual upbringing or a diseased society. It is a possibility for apparently decent people, under certain circumstances.

Perhaps the most famous experiment of this type is Philip Zimbardo's Stanford Prison Experiment, in which he found that subjects randomly cast in the roles of prison guard and prisoner began to behave differently almost right away. The prisoners became passive and depressed; the guards used their power to humiliate and stigmatize. Zimbardo's experiment was badly designed in a number of ways. For example, he gave elaborate instructions to the guards, telling them that their goal should be to induce feelings of alienation and despair in the prisoners. As a consequence, the findings are less than conclusive.[17] Nonetheless, his findings are at least highly suggestive and, when combined with the large amount of other data, corroborate the idea that people who are not individually pathological can behave very badly to others when their situation has been badly designed.

So, we have to look at two things: the individual, and the situation. Situations are not the only things that matter, for research does find individual differences, and the experiments are also plausibly interpreted as showing the influence of widely shared human psychological tendencies. So we need, ultimately, to do what Gandhi did and look deeply into the psychology of the individual, asking what we can do to help compassion and empathy win the clash over fear and hate. But situations matter too, and imperfect people will no doubt act much worse when placed in structures of certain types.

What structures are pernicious? Research suggests several.[18] First, people behave badly when they are not held personally accountable. People act much worse under shelter of anonymity, as parts of a faceless mass, than they do when they are watched and made accountable as individuals. (Anyone who has ever violated the speed limit, and then slowed down on seeing a police car in the rear-view mirror, will know how pervasive this phenomenon is.)

Second, people behave badly when nobody raises a critical voice. Asch's subjects went along with the erroneous judgment when all the other people whom they took to be fellow experimental subjects (and who were really working for the experimenter) concurred in error; but if even one dissenter said something different, they were freed to follow their own perception and judgment.

Third, people behave badly when the human beings over whom they have power are dehumanized and de-individualized. In a wide range of situations, people behave much worse when the "other" is portrayed as like an animal, or as bearing only a number rather than a name. This research intersects with Kindlon and Thompson's clinical observations. Young men anxiously bent on control learned to think of women as mere objects to be manipulated, and this ability to "objectify" women—encouraged by many aspects of our media and Internet culture—further fed their fantasies of domination.

Obviously enough, these situational features can to some extent become part of a basic education—that is, an education process can strengthen the sense of personal accountability, the tendency to see others as distinct individuals, and the willingness to raise a critical voice. We probably cannot produce people who are firm against every manipulation, but we can produce a social culture that is itself a powerful surrounding "situation," strengthening the tendencies that militate against stigmatization and domination. For example, a surrounding culture can teach children to see new immigrant groups, or foreigners, as a faceless mass that threatens their hegemony—or it can teach the perception of the members of these groups as individuals equal to themselves, sharing common rights and responsibilities.

Schools are but one influence on the growing mind and heart of the child. Much of the work of overcoming narcissism and developing concern has to be done in families; and relationships in the peer culture also play a powerful role. Schools, however, can either reinforce or undermine the achievements of the family, good and bad. They can also shape the peer culture. What they provide, through their curricular content and their pedagogy, can greatly affect the developing child's mind.

What lessons does this analysis suggest as we ask what schools can and should do to produce citizens in and for a healthy democracy?

- Develop students' capacity to see the world from the viewpoint of other people, particularly those whom their society tends to portray as lesser, as "mere objects"

- Teach attitudes toward human weakness and helplessness that suggest that weakness is not shameful and the need for others not unmanly; teach children not to be ashamed of need and incompleteness but to see these as occasions for cooperation and reciprocity

- Develop the capacity for genuine concern for others, both near and distant

- Undermine the tendency to shrink from minorities of various kinds in disgust, thinking of them as "lower" and "contaminating"

- Teach real and true things about other groups (racial, religious, and sexual minorities; people with disabilities), so as to counter stereotypes and the disgust that often goes with them

- Promote accountability by treating each child as a responsible agent

- Vigorously promote critical thinking, the skill and courage it requires to raise a dissenting voice.

This is a huge agenda. It must be implemented with constant awareness of local social circumstances, with rich knowledge of local social problems and resources. And it must be addressed not only through educational content but also through pedagogy, to which we turn next.

IV

Socratic Pedagogy: The Importance of Argument

I am a sort of gadfly, given to the democracy by the gods, and the democracy is a large, noble horse who is sluggish in its motions, and requires to be stung into life.

—Socrates, in Plato, *Apology*, 30E

Our mind does not gain true freedom by acquiring materials for knowledge and possessing other people's ideas but by forming its own standards of judgment and producing its own thoughts.

—Rabindranath Tagore, in a syllabus
for a class in his school, c. 1915

Socrates proclaimed that "the unexamined life is not worth living for a human being." In a democracy fond of impassioned rhetoric and skeptical of argument, he lost his life for his allegiance to this ideal of critical questioning. Today his example is central to the theory and practice of liberal education in the Western tradition, and related ideas have been central to ideas of liberal education in India and other non-Western cultures. One of the reasons people have insisted on giving all undergraduates a set of courses in philosophy and other subjects in the humanities is that they believe such courses, through both content and pedagogy, will stimulate students to think and argue for themselves, rather than defer to tradition and authority—and they believe that the ability to argue in this Socratic way is, as Socrates proclaimed, valuable for democracy.

The Socratic ideal, however, is under severe strain in a world bent on maximizing economic growth. The ability to think and argue for oneself looks to many people like something dispensable if what we want are marketable outputs of a quantifiable nature. Furthermore, it is difficult to measure Socratic ability through standardized tests. Only a much more nuanced qualitative assessment of classroom interactions and student writing could tell us to what extent students have learned skills of critical argument. To the extent that standardized tests become the norm by which schools are measured, then, Socratic aspects of both curriculum and pedagogy are likely to be left behind. The economic growth culture has a fondness for standardized tests, and an impatience with pedagogy and content that are not easily assessed in this way. To the extent that personal or national wealth is the focus of the curriculum, Socratic abilities are likely to be underdeveloped.

Why does this matter? Think about the Athenian democracy in which Socrates grew up. In many respects its institutions were admirable, offering all citizens the chance to debate issues of public importance and insisting on citizen participation both in voting and in the jury system. Indeed, Athens went much further toward direct democracy than any modern society in that all major offices, apart from the commander of the army, were filled by lottery. Even though participation in the Assembly was to some extent limited by labor and residence, with urban and leisured citizens playing a disproportionate role—not to mention the exclusion of noncitizens, such as women, slaves, and foreigners—it was still possible for a non-elite male to join in and offer something to the public debate. Why did Socrates think that this thriving democracy was a sluggish horse that needed to be stung into greater wakefulness by the skills of argument that he purveyed?

If we look at political debate—as portrayed, for example, in Thucydides' *History of the Peloponnesian War*—we find that people did not reason with one another very well. Rarely if ever did they examine their major policy objectives, or systematically ask how the diverse things they valued could fit together. Thus we see that the first problem with lack of self-examination is that it leads to unclarity about goals. Plato illustrates this problem vividly in the dialogue *Laches*, when he shows that two of Athens's leading generals, Laches and Nicias, cannot give an account of military courage, even though they think they have it. They simply are not sure whether courage requires thinking about what is worth fighting for, what is ultimately in the city's interest. When Socrates proposes this idea, they like it, and yet their prior thinking had not incorporated it securely. Their utter confusion about one of their own central values might do no harm in a context in which decision-making is easy. With tough choices, however, it is good to be clear about what one wants and cares about, and Plato plausibly links their lack of self-scrutiny with the disastrous military and policy blunders of the subsequent Sicilian expedition, where Nicias was the chief architect of the bruising Athenian defeat. Socratic examination does not guarantee a good set of goals, but it at least guarantees that the goals pursued will be seen clearly in relation to one another, and crucial issues will not be missed by haste and inadvertence.

Another problem with people who fail to examine themselves is that they often prove all too easily influenced. When a talented demagogue addressed the Athenians with moving rhetoric but bad arguments, they were all too ready to be swayed, without ever examining the argument. Then they could easily be swayed back again to the opposite position, without ever sorting out where they really wanted to stand. Thucydides provides a vivid example of this in the debate over the fate of the rebellious colonists of Mytilene. Under the influence of the demagogue Cleon, who speaks to them of slighted honor, the Assembly votes to kill all the men of Mytilene and to enslave the women and children. The city sends out a ship with that order. Then another orator, Diodotus, calms the people and urges mercy. Persuaded, the city votes to rescind the order, and a second ship is sent out with orders to stop the first. By sheer chance, the first ship is becalmed at sea and the second one is able to catch up to it. So, many lives, and such an important policy matter, were left to chance rather than reasoned debate. If Socrates had gotten these people to stop, reflect, and analyze Cleon's speech, and to think critically about what he was urging, at least some would likely have resisted his powerful rhetoric and dissented from his call to violence, without needing Diodotus's calming speech.

Irresolution is frequently compounded by deference to authority and peer pressure, a problem endemic to all human societies, as we have seen. When argument is not the focus, people are easily swayed by the fame or cultural prestige of the speaker, or by the fact that the peer culture is going along. Socratic critical inquiry, by contrast, is utterly unauthoritarian. The status of the speaker does not count; only the nature of the argument. (The slave boy questioned in Plato's *Meno* does better than famous politicians, partly because he is not arrogant.) Teachers of philosophy betray Socrates' legacy if they cast themselves as authority figures. What Socrates brought to Athens was an example of truly democratic vulnerability and humility. Class, fame, and prestige count for nothing, and the argument counts for all.

Nor does the peer group count. The Socratic arguer is a confirmed dissenter because she knows that it is just each person and the argument wrestling things out. The numbers of people who think this or that make no difference. Someone trained to follow argument rather than numbers is a good person for a democracy to have, the sort of person who would stand up against the pressure to say something false or hasty that Asch's experiments demonstrate.

A further problem with people who lead the unexamined life is that they often treat one another disrespectfully. When people think that political debate is something like an athletic contest, where the aim is to score points for their own side, they are likely to see the "other side" as the enemy and to wish its defeat, or even humiliation. It would not occur to them to seek compromise or to find common ground, any more than in a hockey match the Chicago Blackhawks would seek "common ground" with their adversaries. Socrates' attitude toward his interlocutors, by contrast, is exactly the same as his attitude toward himself. Everyone needs examination, and all are equal in the face of the argument. This critical attitude uncovers the structure of each person's position, in the process uncovering shared assumptions, points of intersection that can help fellow citizens progress to a shared conclusion.

Consider the case of Billy Tucker, a nineteen-year-old student in a business college in Massachusetts who was required to take a series of "liberal arts" courses, including one in philosophy.[1] Interestingly, his instructor, Krishna Mallick, was an Indian American originally from Kolkata, familiar with Tagore's educational ideal and a fine practitioner of it, so his class stood at the intersection of two highly Socratic cultures. Students in her class began by learning about the life and death of Socrates; Tucker was strangely moved by this man who would give up life itself for the pursuit of the argument. Then the students learned a little formal logic, and Tucker was delighted to find that he got a high score on a test in this subject; he had never thought he could do well in something abstract and intellectual. Next, they analyzed political speeches and editorials, looking for logical flaws. Finally, in the last phase of the course, they did research for debates on issues of the day. Tucker was surprised to discover that he was being asked to argue against the death penalty, although he actually favored it. He had never understood, he said, that one could produce arguments for a position that one does not hold oneself. He told me that this experience gave him a new attitude toward political discussion: Now he is more inclined to respect the opposing position and to be curious about the arguments on both sides, and what the two sides might share, rather than seeing the discussion as simply a way of making boasts and assertions. We can see how this humanizes the political "other," making the mind see the opposing person as a rational being who may share at least some thoughts with one's own group.

Let us now consider the relevance of this ability to the current state of modern pluralistic democracies surrounded by a powerful global marketplace. First of all, we can report that, even if we were just aiming at economic success, leading corporate executives understand very well the importance of creating a corporate culture in which critical voices are not silenced, a culture of both individuality and accountability. Leading business educators with whom I have spoken in the United States say that they trace some of our biggest disasters—the failures of certain phases of the NASA space shuttle program, the even more disastrous failures of Enron and WorldCom—to a culture of yes-people, where authority and peer pressure ruled the roost and critical ideas were never articulated. (A recent confirmation of this idea is Malcolm Gladwell's study of the culture of airline pilots, which finds that deference to authority is a major predictor of compromised safety.)[2]

A second issue in business is innovation, and there are reasons to suppose that a liberal arts education strengthens the skills of imagining and independent thinking that are crucial to maintaining a successful culture of innovation. Again, leading business educators typically urge students to pursue a broad-based program and to develop their imaginations, and many firms prefer liberal arts graduates to those with a narrower training. Although it is difficult to construct a controlled experiment on such an issue, it does seem that one of the distinctive features of American economic strength is the fact that we have relied on a general liberal arts education and, in the sciences, on basic scientific education and research, rather than focusing more narrowly on applied skills. These issues deserve a full exploration, and it seems likely that, once fully investigated, they will yield further strong support for my recommendations.

But, we have said, the goal of democracies that want to remain stable cannot and should not be simply economic growth, so let us now return to our central topic, political culture. As we have seen, human beings are prone to be subservient to both authority and peer pressure; to prevent atrocities we need to counteract these tendencies, producing a culture of individual dissent. Asch, we recall, found that when even one person in his study group stood up for the truth, others followed, demonstrating that one critical voice can have significant consequences. By emphasizing each person's active voice, we also promote a culture of accountability. When people see their ideas as their own responsibility, they are more likely, too, to see their deeds as their own responsibility. That was essentially the point Tagore made in *Nationalism* when he insisted that the bureaucratization of social life and the relentless machinelike character of modern states had deadened people's moral imaginations, leading them to acquiesce in atrocities with no twinge of conscience. Independence of thought, he added, is crucial if the world is not to be led headlong toward destruction. In his lecture in Japan in 1917, he spoke of a "gradual suicide through shrinkage of the soul," observing that people more and more permitted themselves to be used as parts in a giant machine and to carry out the projects of national power. Only a robustly critical public culture could possibly stop this baneful trend.

Socratic thinking is important in any democracy. But it is particularly important in societies that need to come to grips with the presence of people who differ by ethnicity, caste, and religion. The idea that one will take responsibility for one's own reasoning, and exchange ideas with others in an atmosphere of mutual respect for reason, is essential to the peaceful resolution of differences, both within a nation and in a world increasingly polarized by ethnic and religious conflict.

Socratic thinking is a social practice. Ideally it ought to shape the functioning of a wide range of social and political institutions. Since our topic is formal education, however, we can see that it is also a discipline. It can be taught as part of a school or college curriculum. It will not be well taught, however, unless it informs the spirit of classroom pedagogy and the school's entire ethos. Each student must be treated as an individual whose powers of mind are unfolding and who is expected to make an active and creative contribution to classroom discussion. This sort of pedagogy is impossible without small classes, or, at the very least, regular meetings of small sections within larger classes.

But how, more specifically, can a liberal education teach Socratic values? At the college and university level, the answer to this question is reasonably well understood. As a starting point, critical thinking should be infused into the pedagogy of classes of many types, as students learn to probe, to evaluate evidence, to write papers with well-structured arguments, and to analyze the arguments presented to them in other texts.

It seems likely, however, that a more focused attention to the structure of argument is essential if these relatively mature students are to get the full immersion in active Socratic thinking that a liberal arts education makes possible. For this reason, I have argued that all colleges and universities should follow the lead of America's Catholic colleges and universities, which require at least two semesters of philosophy, in addition to whatever theology or religious courses are required.[3] The course Tucker took at Bentley College is one good example of the way in which such a course might be constructed. Typically, some philosophical texts will provide a jumping-off point—and the dialogues of Plato are second to none for their capacity to inspire searching, active thinking, with the life and example of Socrates up front to inspire. Tucker's course also paid attention to formal logical structure, and this is very useful, because it gives students templates that they can then apply to texts of many different types, from newspaper editorials and political speeches to their own arguments about issues they care about. Finally, getting students to practice what they have learned by debating in class and writing papers—all with detailed feedback from the instructor—allows them to internalize and master what they have learned.

There is no doubt that even well-prepared college undergraduates need this type of class in order to develop more fully their capacities for citizenship and respectful political interaction. Even smart and well-prepared students do not usually learn to take apart an argument without patient training. Such teaching, still relatively common in the United States, demands a great deal from faculty, and cannot be done simply through large lectures. This sort of intensive exchange with undergraduates is difficult to find in most European and Asian countries, where students enter university to read a single subject and do not have liberal arts requirements in the first place, and where the normal mode of teaching involves large lectures with little or no active participation by students and little or no feedback on student writing, a theme to which I shall return in the final chapter.

Tucker was already a high school graduate, but it is possible, and essential, to encourage Socratic thinking from the very beginning of a child's education. Indeed, this has often been done. It is one of the hallmarks of modern progressive education.

AT THIS POINT, we need to pause and think historically, since valuable models of Socratic education have long been developed, as a reaction against passive learning, in a wide variety of countries, and these can and should inform our search. Examining this rich and continuous tradition will give us reference points for further analysis and theoretical sources to enrich it.

Starting in the eighteenth century, thinkers in Europe, North America, and, prominently, India began to break away from the model of education as rote learning and to pursue experiments in which the child was an active and critical participant. These experiments unfolded in different places to some extent independently, but eventually with a lot of mutual influence and borrowing. Socrates was an inspirational figure in all of these reform movements, but they were also inspired, and perhaps more so, by the sheer deadness of existing schools, and by educators' feeling that rote learning and student passivity could not be good for citizenship or for life.

These school experiments all involved more than Socratic questioning. Much of what they proposed will concern us later, when we turn to world citizenship, and, especially, to play and the arts. In this chapter, we will need to lay out the basic ideas of each reform as a whole, in order to convey an overarching sense of each reformer's aims, giving ourselves a framework within which to investigate the idea of critical thinking. As we do this, however, we shall then focus on the Socratic component of each thinker's proposal, returning to other aspects of the education in chapters 5 and 6.

In Europe, a touchstone for all these experiments was Jean-Jacques Rousseau's great work *Emile* (1762), which describes an education aimed at rendering the young man autonomous, capable of his own independent thought and of solving practical problems on his own, without reliance on authority. Rousseau held that the ability to navigate in the world by one's own wits was a key aspect of making a child a good citizen who could live on terms of equality with others, rather than making them his servants. A great deal of Emile's education is therefore practical, and he learns by doing, a hallmark of all subsequent experiments in progressive education. The Socratic element is also prominent, however, as Emile is told nothing on authority from his teacher, but has to puzzle things out for himself, while the teacher simply probes and questions.

Rousseau did not set up a school, and *Emile* tells us little about what a good one might be like, since it depicts a single child with a tutor. In this sense, it is a profoundly nonpractical work, albeit philosophically deep. I shall therefore not dwell on the details of Rousseau's rather schematic philosophical account, preferring to focus on real educational experiments inspired by it. For Rousseau's ideas greatly influenced two European thinkers whose lives overlapped with his and who did establish schools in accordance with their views.

Swiss educator Johann Pestalozzi (1746–1827) took as his target the practice of rote learning and force-feeding, ubiquitous in schools of his day. The purpose of this sort of education, as he portrays it, was the creation of docile citizens who, as grown-ups, would follow authority and not ask questions. In his copious writings on education, some of them in fictional form, Pestalozzi describes, by contrast, an education aimed at rendering the child active and inquisitive through the development of his or her natural critical capacities. He presents the Socratic type of education as engaging and enlivening, and as just plain common sense—if one's goal is to train the mind, and not to produce herdlike obedience.

Pestalozzi's was not a narrow Socratism—he also gave significance, in education, to sympathy and affection. His ideal teacher was a maternal figure, as well as a Socratic challenger. He was ahead of his era in urging a complete ban on corporal punishment, and he emphasized the importance of play in early education. We should bear this larger context in mind as we study his Socratic proposals, although we shall investigate it further only in chapter 6.

In the influential novel *Leonard and Gertrude* (1781), Pestalozzi describes the reform of education in a small town, from an elite sort of indoctrination to a highly participatory and democratic form of mental awakening. Significantly, the agent of this radical change is a working-class woman, Gertrude, who exemplifies the maternal, the inquisitive, and the down-to-earth, all in one. In her village school she educates boys and girls from all social classes, treating them as equals and teaching them useful practical skills. ("Surely it is human beings we are educating, not brilliant mushroom growths," Pestalozzi at one point nicely observes.)

As with Emile's tutor, Gertrude gets the children to solve problems for themselves—Pestalozzi is the inventor of the concept of the "object lesson"—and she always encourages active questioning. Unlike Socrates, however, and to some extent unlike Rousseau's imaginary tutor, Gertrude is also affectionate and interested in cultivating the children's emotional capacities along with their capacity for criticism. In the 1801 book *How Gertrude Teaches Her Children*, Pestalozzi summarizes the principles of good schooling, making it clear that family love is the source and the animating principle of all true education. He suggests that young men and women should both become more maternal and loving; princes, he suggests, have made people aggressive for their own selfish ends, but human nature is in its essence maternal, and this maternal care is the "sacred source of patriotism and civic virtue." The Socratic element in Pestalozzi must always be understood in connection with this focus on emotional development.

Pestalozzi was too radical for his time and place; the various schools he started were all failures, and Napoleon, whom he approached, refused to take an interest in his ideas. Ultimately, however, he had a great influence on educational practice, as people from all over Europe came to visit and talk with him. His influence extended to the United States, and both Bronson Alcott and Horace Mann owe much to his ideas.

Slightly later, German educator Friedrich Froebel (1782–1852) conducted reforms of early education, in the spirit of Pestalozzi, that have changed the way young children in virtually all the world's countries begin their schooling. For Froebel was the founder and theorist of the "kindergarten," the year before "regular" schooling begins in which children are gently encouraged to expand their cognitive faculties in an atmosphere of play and affection, and one that, in a Socratic spirit, emphasizes children's own activity as the source of their learning. Like Pestalozzi, Froebel intensely disliked traditional models of education that viewed children as passive vessels into which the wisdom of the ages would be poured. He believed that education should focus on eliciting and cultivating the child's natural abilities through supportive play. The idea of the kindergarten is just this idea of a place where one learns and unfolds through play. Froebel has a lot of mystical views about the properties of certain physical objects, the so-called Froebel gifts: for example, the ball. By manipulating these symbolic objects, children learn to think actively and to master their environment. Modern kindergartens wisely leave Froebel's more mystical flights to one side, while retaining the core idea that children learn to unfold themselves by active thought, reciprocity, and the active manipulation of objects. Froebel believes that aggression is a reaction to natural helplessness and will drop away of its own accord when children learn to cope with the world around them, while their natural capacity for sympathy and reciprocity will be extended. In terms of our narrative of child development this is a bit too sanguine, but it goes in the right direction.

Because Froebel is concerned with extremely young children, Socratic techniques are not presented in any formal way, but their basis is firmly laid, by encouraging the child to be active, exploring and questioning rather than merely receiving. His idea that each child deserves respect, and that each (regardless of class or gender) should be an inquirer, is also thoroughly Socratic. Children all over the world today owe much to his contribution, since the idea of a type of early education through play in an environment of sympathy and love has created kindergartens more or less everywhere. This healthy idea is under pressure in our world, as children are pressed to drill at skills earlier and earlier in life, often losing opportunities to learn through relaxed playing.

Now our historical search moves to America, where European progressive reforms had a large and formative influence—perhaps explaining why the idea of liberal arts education has flourished here as it has not in Europe. Bronson Alcott (1799–1888) is best known today as the father of novelist Louisa May Alcott, and his school is lovingly depicted in her novels *Little Men* and *Jo's Boys*. Louisa depicts her father (represented as Jo's husband, Professor Bhaer) as following "the Socratic method of instruction"; he mentions that he is strongly influenced by Pestalozzi and Froebel. This appears to be an accurate characterization of Bronson Alcott's orientation, although we must add to these influences that of German idealism and the poetry of Wordsworth.

At the Temple School in Boston, founded in 1834, Alcott taught thirty boys and girls, ages six to twelve. (Teachers, too, were both female and male.) In 1839 the school admitted a black pupil; many parents withdrew their children, and the school closed. But during its brief existence, it carried on and extended the legacy of European progressive education. Alcott's methods are even more clearly Socratic than those of Pestalozzi and Froebel. Instruction always took the form of questions rather than assertions, as children were urged to examine themselves, both their thoughts and their emotions. "Education," he wrote, "is that process by which thought is opened out of the soul, and, associated with outward things, is reflected back upon itself and thus made conscious of the reality and shape [of things]. . . . It is self-realization." This is the language of Hegel, more than of Plato, but the bottom line, in terms of pedagogy, is Socratic. Education proceeds by questioning and self-scrutiny.

Like Froebel and Pestalozzi, Alcott diverged from Socrates in emphasizing emotional development and the role of poetry; classes often focused on the reading and interpretation of poems, Wordsworth being a particular favorite. Argument, however, was not slighted, and children were taught to take responsibility for defending their own ideas. For Alcott, as for his European predecessors, Socrates' approach is incomplete because it does not attend to the emotions and the imagination. Nonetheless, Socrates supplied a major part of what all sought: an emphasis on self-examination, personal accountability, and individual mental activity as antidotes to an education that formed students into pliant tools of traditional authority.

I shall pass more rapidly over a figure of considerable historical significance, Horace Mann (1796–1859). A contemporary of

Alcott's, but in some respects more politically mainstream, Mann might be the most influential figure in the history of American public education, before Dewey. Beginning with his pathbreaking reforms in the Massachusetts public schools, and ending with his work at Antioch College, which he founded, Mann, an abolitionist and a leading defender of women's equality, always stood for inclusiveness: for a liberal education (not just manual training) for everyone, without cost; for free libraries all over the state; and for high standards of teaching in the schools that non-elite pupils attended. As with the figures we have considered, then, Mann was a reformer who detested mere rote learning. His reforms were closely linked to an egalitarian and inclusive conception of democracy. He held that no democracy can endure unless its citizens are educated and active. In matters of inclusion, he was a radical, insisting on equal education of all children regardless of race or sex, on a serious attempt to eradicate class distinctions in education, and even (at Antioch) on equal pay for women in faculty positions. It was under his influence that Massachusetts, in 1852, passed the first state law requiring compulsory school attendance.

In some respects, Mann also shared pedagogical ideas with our earlier reformers; he rejected ineffective and authoritarian methods of teaching, seeking understanding rather than routine. His emphasis, however, was typically on basic competence, literacy, and numeracy; and his critique of authoritarian teachers (especially dogmatic religious teachers who based their teaching on the Bible) was therefore somewhat limited, focusing on the evident nonsuccess of such methods in teaching reading and writing. His insistence on getting children to understand what they were reading was defended less by appeal to the intrinsic worth of questioning and reflection than by pointing to the fact that children simply cannot learn reading by imitation, without understanding.

At Antioch, toward the end of his life, his radical inclusiveness continued (Antioch was the first U.S. college to educate women and men as full equals, and one of the first to educate black students and white students as equals). Meanwhile, his Socratic commitments became clearer: Antioch was the first college to emphasize classroom discussion, and it even offered independent study under faculty guidance.

Mann, in short, was a great practical reformer and a powerful champion of democratic educaton. At least where the schools were concerned, however, he focused above all on basic skills, and his commitment to Socratic and democratic values in the classroom was less central and less reflective than that of the other figures our historical excursus has discussed. With regret, we shall therefore leave him at this point and turn to a thinker who brought Socrates into virtually every American classroom.

Undoubtedly the most influential and theoretically distinguished American practitioner of Socratic education, John Dewey (1869–1952) changed the way virtually all American schools understand their task. Whatever the defects of American primary and secondary education, it is generally understood that stuffing children full of facts and asking them to regurgitate them does not add up to an education; children need to learn to take charge of their own thinking and to engage with the world in a curious and critical spirit. Dewey was a major philosopher, so, with him as with Rousseau, it will not be possible to go deeply into the elaborate ideas underlying his educational practice, but we can at least get a general idea of the connection he made between democratic citizenship and Socratic education.

Unlike all the theorists we have previously considered, Dewey lived and taught in a thriving democracy, and the production of active, curious, critical, and mutually respectful democratic citizens was his central goal. Despite Dewey's wariness of classical "great books"—because he saw such books turned into authorities, and name-dropping substituted for real intellectual engagement—Socrates remained a source of inspiration for him, because he brought lively rational and critical engagement to democracy. Another important inspiration was Froebel—to the exposition of whose ideas Dewey, rarely fond of writing about his distinguished predecessors, devotes considerable emphasis.[4]

For Dewey, the central problem with conventional methods of education is the passivity it encourages in students. Schools have been treated as places for listening and absorbing, and listening has been preferred to analyzing, sifting, and active problem-solving. Asking students to be passive listeners not only fails to develop their active critical faculties, it positively weakens them: "[T]he child approaches the book without intellectual hunger, without alertness, without a questioning attitude, and the result is the one so deplorably common: such abject dependence upon books as weakens and cripples vigor of thought and inquiry." Such a subservient attitude, bad for life in general, is fatal for democracy, since democracies will not survive without alert and active citizens. Instead of listening, then, the child should always be doing: figuring things out, thinking about them, raising questions. The change he wanted was, he said, "the change from more or less passive and inert recipiency and restraint to one of buoyant outgoing energy."[5]

The best way of rendering young people active, Dewey believed, was to make a classroom a real-world space continuous with the world outside—a place where real problems are debated, real practical skills evoked. Thus Socratic questioning was not just an intellectual skill, it was an aspect of practical engagement, a stance toward problems in real life. It was also a way of engaging with others, and Dewey always stressed the fact that in a good school pupils learn skills of citizenship by undertaking common projects and solving them together, in a respectful and yet critical spirit. Cooperative activity had, he believed, the additional dividend of teaching respect for manual labor and other trades; conventional schools often encourage an elitist preference for sedentary occupations. So Dewey's Socratism was not a sit-at-your-desk-and-argue technique; it was a form of life carried on with other children in the pursuit of an understanding of real-world issues and immediate practical projects, under the guidance of teachers, but without imposition of authority from without.

Typically, students would begin with a specific and immediate practical task: to cook something, or weave something, or maintain a garden. In the course of solving these immediate problems, they would be led to many questions: Where do these materials come from? Who made them? By what forms of labor did they reach me? How should we think about the social organization of these forms of labor? (Why is cotton so difficult to prepare for weaving? How did these practical problems interact with slave labor? Questions might fan out in many directions.)[6]

In short, the Socratic questioning grows from a real event, as children are led to treat these events, and their own activity, as "points of departure."[7] At the same time, by learning that producing cotton thread connects to all these complicated questions, children understand the complex significance of manual labor itself, and learn a new attitude toward it. Above all, children are learning through their own (social) activity, not by passively receiving; they thus model, and learn, citizenship. Dewey's experiments have left a profound mark on early education in America, as has his emphasis on the interconnectedness of the world, which we shall discuss in chapter 5, and his focus on the arts, which we shall discuss in chapter 6.

I have spoken so far of a Socratic method that had wide influence in Europe and North America. It would be wrong, however, to think that a Socratic approach to early education was found only there. Rabindranath Tagore in India conducted a closely related experiment, founding a school in Santiniketan, outside Kolkata, and, later, as mentioned, a liberal arts university, Visva-Bharati, to go with it. Tagore was far from being the only experimental educator in India in the early twentieth century. A similar progressive elementary school was set up in connection with Jamia Millia Islamia, a liberal university founded by Muslims who believed that their own Quranic tradition mandated Socratic learning.[8] All these experiments are closely connected to reforms of traditional laws and customs regarding women and children, such as raising the age of consent to marriage, giving women access to higher education, and, ultimately, giving them full citizenship in the new nation. Such reform movements existed in many regions. Tagore's experiment, however, was the most widely influential of these attempts, so I shall focus on it.

Tagore, who won the Nobel Prize for Literature in 1913, was one of those rare people who have world-class gifts in many different areas. He won the prize for his poetry, but he was also a superb novelist, short-story writer, and playwright. More remarkable, he was a painter whose work is valued more highly with the passing years, a composer who wrote more than two thousand songs, which are immensely loved in Bengali culture today—including songs later adopted as the national anthems of both India and Bangladesh—and a choreographer whose work was studied by founders of modern dance such as Isadora Duncan (whose dance idiom also influenced his) and whose dance dramas were eagerly sought out by European and American dancers who spent time at his school. Tagore was also an impressive philosopher, whose book *Nationalism* (1917) is a major contribution to thought about the modern state, and whose *The Religion of Man* (1930) argues that humanity can make progress only by cultivating its capacity for a more inclusive sympathy, and that this capacity can be cultivated only by an education that emphasizes global learning, the arts, and Socratic self-criticism. All these aspects of Tagore's genius made their way into the plan and daily life of his school. It was, perhaps above all, the school of a poet and artist, someone who understood how central the arts all are to the whole development of the personality.[9] Although this aspect of the school will occupy us only later, in chapter 6, it is important to bear in mind that it established the context within which his Socratic experiment unfolded. Both the Socratic and the artistic aspects of the school were inspired by a hatred of dead and imprisoning traditions that kept both men and women, as he saw it, from realizing their full human potential.

Tagore, like many people of his social class, was learned in Western thought and literature. (He translated Shakespeare's *Macbeth* into Bengali at the age of fifteen.) His educational philosophy may well have been influenced a bit by Rousseau, and a lot of his thought shows the influence of cosmopolitan French thinker Auguste Comte (1798–1857), who also influenced John Stuart Mill, who wrote an entire book about Comte.[10] Thus we could call Tagore and Mill cousins: Tagore's idea of the "religion of man" is similar to Mill's notion of a "religion of humanity," and both have their roots in Comte's idea of inclusive human sympathy. Tagore and Mill had a similar hatred of the tyranny of custom, and both were energetic proponents of individual liberty.

If Tagore was influenced by some Western thinking, however, influence went, even more clearly, in the other direction. His school was visited by countless artists, dancers, writers, and educators from Europe and North America who took his ideas home with them. He met and corresponded with Maria Montessori, who visited Santiniketan to observe his experiments. Leonard Elmhirst spent some years at Tagore's school, and then, returning to Britain, founded the progressive arts-oriented Dartington Hall, a school that is still a beacon of the type of education I am defending. Tagore may also have influenced John Dewey. Although such links are difficult to trace because Dewey rarely describes his influences, we know that Tagore spent extended periods in Illinois (visiting his son, who was studying agriculture at the University of Illinois) at just the time Dewey was establishing his Laboratory School. At any rate, whether there was influence or not, the ideas of the two men about critical thinking and the arts are closely related.

Tagore hated every school he ever attended, and he left them all as quickly as possible. What he hated was rote learning and the treatment of the pupil as a passive vessel of received cultural values. Tagore's novels, stories, and dramas are obsessed with the need to challenge the past, to be alive to a wide range of possibilities. He once expressed his views about rote learning in an allegory about traditional education called "The Parrot's Training."[11]

A certain Raja has a beautiful parrot, and he becomes convinced that it needs to be educated, so he summons wise people from all over his empire. They argue endlessly about methodology and especially about textbooks. "Textbooks can never be too many for our purpose!" they say. The bird gets a beautiful school building: a golden cage. The learned teachers show the Raja the impressive method of instruction they have devised. "The method was so stupendous that the bird looked ridiculously unimportant in comparison." And so, "With textbook in one hand and baton in the other, the pundits [learned teachers] gave the poor bird what may fitly be called lessons!"

One day the bird dies. Nobody notices for quite some time. The Raja's nephews come to report the fact:

> The nephews said, "Sire, the bird's education has been completed."
> "Does it hop?" the Raja enquired.
> "Never!" said the nephews.
> "Does it fly?"
> "No."
> "Bring me the bird," said the Raja.
> The bird was brought to him. . . . The Raja poked its body with his finger. Only its inner stuffing of book-leaves rustled.
> Outside the window, the murmur of the spring breeze amongst the newly budded asoka leaves made the April morning wistful.

The students of Tagore's school at Santiniketan had no such sad fate. Their entire education nourished the ability to think for oneself and to become a dynamic participant in cultural and political choice, rather than simply a follower of tradition. And Tagore was particularly sensitive to the unequal burden dead customs imposed upon women. Indeed, most of the searching questioners in his plays and stories are women, since dissatisfaction with their lot prods them to challenge and to think. In his dance-drama *The Land of Cards*, all the inhabitants of that land act robotically, playing out two-dimensional lives in ways defined by the card-picture they wear—until the women begin to think and question. So Tagore's Socratism, like his choreography, is shaped by his passionate defense of women's empowerment, as well as by his own unhappy experience in old-fashioned schools.

The school Tagore founded was in many ways highly unconventional. Almost all classes were held outside. The arts were woven through the whole curriculum, and, as mentioned, gifted artists and writers flocked to the school to take part in the experiment. But Socratic questioning was front and center, both in the curriculum and in the pedagogy. Students were encouraged to deliberate about decisions that governed their daily life and to take the initiative in organizing meetings. Syllabi describe the school, repeatedly, as a self-governing community in which children are encouraged to seek intellectual self-reliance and freedom. In one syllabus, Tagore writes: "The mind will receive its impressions . . . by full freedom given for inquiry and experience and at the same time will be stimulated to think for itself. . . . Our mind does not gain true freedom by acquiring materials for knowledge and possessing other people's ideas but by forming its own standards of judgment and producing its own thoughts."[12] Accounts of his practice report that he repeatedly put problems before the students and elicited answers from them by questioning, in Socratic fashion.

Another device Tagore used to stimulate Socratic questioning was role-playing, as children were invited to step outside their own point of view and inhabit that of another person. This gave them the freedom to experiment with other intellectual positions and to understand them from within. Here we begin to see the close link Tagore forged between Socratic questioning and imaginative empathy: Arguing in Socratic fashion requires the ability to understand other positions from within, and this understanding often provides new incentives to challenge tradition in a Socratic way.

OUR HISTORICAL DIGRESSION has shown us a living tradition that uses Socratic values to produce a certain type of citizen: active, critical, curious, capable of resisting authority and peer pressure. These historical examples show us what has been done, but not what we should or can do here and now, in the elementary and secondary schools of today. The examples of Pestalozzi, Alcott, and Tagore are helpful, but extremely general. They do not tell today's average teacher very much about how to structure learning so that it elicits and develops the child's ability to understand the logical structure of an argument, to detect bad reasoning, to challenge ambiguity—in short, to do, at an age-appropriate level, what Tucker's teachers did in his college-level course. Indeed, one of the great defects of Tagore's experiment—shared to some degree by Pestalozzi and Alcott—was that he prescribed no method that others could carry on in his absence. Prescribing is, of course, a delicate matter when what one wants to produce is freedom from the dead hand of authority. Froebel and Dewey offer more definite guidance because they do not simply theorize, they also recommend some general procedures in early education that others in different times and places have imitated and recast with great success. Dewey, however, never addressed systematically the question of how Socratic critical reasoning might be taught to children of various ages. Thus, his proposals remain general and in need of supplementation by the actual classroom teacher who may or may not be prepared to bring this approach to life.[13]

But teachers who want to teach Socratically have a contemporary source of practical guidance (which, of course, must be only part of an overall program to structure a Socratic classroom in which children are, throughout the day, active and curious participants). They can find very useful and yet nondictatorial advice about Socratic pedagogy in a series of books produced by philosopher Matthew Lipman, whose Philosophy for Children curriculum was developed at the Institute for the Advancement of Philosophy for Children at Montclair State College in New Jersey. Lipman begins from the conviction that young children are active, questioning beings whose capacity to probe and inquire ought to be respected and further developed—a starting point that he shares with the European progressive tradition. He and his colleague philosopher Gareth Matthews share, as well, the view that children are capable of interesting philosophical thought, that children do not just move in a predetermined way from stage to stage, but actively ponder the big questions of life, and that the insights they come up with must be taken seriously by adults.[14]

Lipman also thinks that children can profit early on from highly specific attention to the logical properties of thought, that they are naturally able to follow logical structure, but that it usually takes guidance and leading to help them develop their capacities. His series of books—in which complex ideas are always presented through engaging stories about children figuring things out for themselves—show again and again how this attention to logical structure pays off in daily life and in countering ill-informed prejudices and stereotypes. Two examples from his first book, *Harry Stottlemeier's Discovery*, will illustrate the basic idea. Harry (whose name, of course, alludes to Aristotle and to Aristotle's discovery—and Harry's—the syllogism) is playing around with sentences, and he makes a discovery: Some sentences cannot be "turned around." It is true that "all oaks are trees," but it is not true that "all trees are oaks." It is true that "all planets revolve about the sun," but it is not true that "all things that revolve about the sun are planets." He tells his discovery to his friend Lisa, but she points out that he is wrong when he says, "You can't turn sentences around." Sentences that start with "No" work differently. "No eagles are lions," but it is equally true that "no lions are eagles." The two friends happily embark on more language games, trying to sort out the terrain for themselves.

Meanwhile, real life obtrudes. Harry's mother is talking to her neighbor Mrs. Olson, who is trying to spread some gossip about a new neighbor, Mrs. Bates. "That Mrs. Bates," she says, ". . . every day I see her go into the liquor store. Now, you know how concerned I am about those unfortunate people who just can't stop drinking. Every day, I see them go into the liquor store. Well, that makes me wonder whether Mrs. Bates is, you know . . ."

Harry has an idea. "Mrs. Olson," he says, "just because, according to you, *all people who can't stop drinking* are *people who go to the liquor store*, that doesn't mean that *all people who go to the liquor store* are *people who can't stop drinking*." Harry's mother reproves him for interrupting, but he can tell from the expression on her face that she is pleased with what he has said.

Logic is real, and it often governs our human relations. Lots of slurs and stereotypes work in exactly this way, through fallacious inference. The ability to detect fallacy is one of the things that makes democratic life decent.

Harry and his friend Tony, with their teacher, are working out the difference between "every" and "only." "Every," like "all," introduces a sentence that cannot be turned around. Tony tells Harry that his father wants him to be an engineer like him because Tony is good in math. Tony feels that there is a problem with his father's argument, but he doesn't know quite what it is. Harry sees it: The fact that "all engineers are people who are good in math" doesn't mean that "all people who are good in math are engineers"—or, the equivalent, that "only engineers are good in math." Tony goes home and points this out to his father, who, luckily, is impressed by his son's acuity rather than annoyed by his failure to like his career advice. He helps Tony draw a picture of the situation; a large circle represents people who are good in math. A smaller circle inside this represents engineers, who are also good in math. But there is room for something else in the large circle, clearly. "You were right," says Tony's father with a faint smile, "you were perfectly right."[15]

All this takes place in the first few pages of the first book in Lipman's series, intended for children ages ten to fourteen. The series contains books that progress in complexity, but also cover different areas: mind, ethics, and so forth. The whole sequence, its rationale, and its pedagogical use are nicely explained in a book for teachers, *Philosophy in the Classroom*, which also discusses teacher training and the bare bones of an M.A. degree program in this area.[16] The series as a whole takes students to the point where they might begin to work through Plato's Socratic dialogues on their own, the point, roughly, where Billy Tucker's class begins, although it can be reached earlier by children with regular exposure to Socratic techniques.

This series is aimed at American children. Part of its appeal is familiarity, and the gentle humor that pervades it; so it will have to be rewritten as culture changes, and different versions will need to be devised in different cultures. What is important is to see that something like this is available, and that the teacher who wants to do what Socrates, Pestalozzi, and Tagore all did need not be an inventive genius like them. Some franchised methods are lifeless and excessively directive in themselves. Some become like this because of misuse. In this case, however, the humor and freshness of the books themselves, and their respect for children, are strong bulwarks against misuse. The books obviously do not constitute a complete Socratic approach to education. The whole ethos of the school and classroom has to be infused with respect for the child's active powers of mind, and for this Dewey is an especially powerful guide. They do, however, supply one component of such an education in an accessible and lively way.

The aspiration to make elementary and secondary classrooms Socratic is not utopian; nor does it require genius. It is well within the reach of any community that respects the minds of its children and the needs of a developing democracy. But what is happening today? Well, in many nations Socrates either was never in fashion or went out of fashion long ago. India's government schools are by and large dreary places of rote learning, untouched by the achievements of Tagore and his fellow Socratic educators. The United States is somewhat better off, because Dewey and his Socratic experiments have had widespread influence. But things are rapidly changing, and my concluding chapter will show how close we are to the collapse of the Socratic ideal.

Democracies all over the world are undervaluing, and consequently neglecting, skills that we all badly need to keep democracies vital, respectful, and accountable.

V

Citizens of the World

And so we have to labour and to work, and work hard, to
give reality to our dreams. Those dreams are for India, but
they are also for the world, for all the nations and peoples are
too closely knit together today for any one of them to imagine
that it can live apart. Peace is said to be indivisible, so is freedom, so is prosperity now, and so also is disaster in this One
World that can no longer be split into isolated fragments.
> —Jawaharlal Nehru, speech on the eve of
> India's independence, 14 August 1947

Suddenly the walls that separated the different races are seen
to have given way, and we find ourselves standing face to face.
> —Tagore, *The Religion of Man*, 1931

We live in a world in which people face one another across gulfs
of geography, language, and nationality. More than at any time
in the past, we all depend on people we have never seen, and
they depend on us. The problems we need to solve—economic,
environmental, religious, and political—are global in their scope.
They have no hope of being solved unless people once distant
come together and cooperate in ways they have not before. Think

of global warming; decent trade regulations; the protection of the environment and animal species; the future of nuclear energy and the dangers of nuclear weapons; the movement of labor and the establishment of decent labor standards; the protection of children from trafficking, sexual abuse, and forced labor. All these can only truly be addressed by multinational discussions. Such a list could be extended almost indefinitely.

Nor do any of us stand outside this global interdependency. The global economy has tied all of us to distant lives. Our simplest decisions as consumers affect the living standard of people in distant nations who are involved in the production of products we use. Our daily lives put pressure on the global environment. It is irresponsible to bury our heads in the sand, ignoring the many ways in which we influence, every day, the lives of distant people. Education, then, should equip us all to function effectively in such discussions, seeing ourselves as "citizens of the world," to use a time-honored phrase, rather than merely as Americans, or Indians, or Europeans.

In the absence of a good grounding for international cooperation in the schools and universities of the world, however, our human interactions are likely to be mediated by the thin norms of market exchange in which human lives are seen primarily as instruments for gain. The world's schools, colleges, and universities therefore have an important and urgent task: to cultivate in students the ability to see themselves as members of a heterogeneous nation (for all modern nations are heterogeneous), and a still more heterogeneous world, and to understand something of the history and character of the diverse groups that inhabit it.

This aspect of education requires a lot of factual knowledge that students who grew up even thirty years ago almost never got, at least in the United States: knowledge about the varied subgroups (ethnic, national, religious, gender based) that comprise one's own nation, their achievements, struggles, and contributions; and similarly complex knowledge about nations and traditions outside one's own. (We always taught young people about small parts of the world, but until very recently, we never tried to cover the major nations and regions in a systematic way, treating all regions as significant.) Knowledge is no guarantee of good behavior, but ignorance is a virtual guarantee of bad behavior. Simple cultural and religious stereotypes abound in our world: for example, the facile equation of Islam with terrorism. The way to begin combating these is to make sure that from a very early age students learn a different relation to the world, mediated by correct facts and respectful curiosity. Young people must gradually come to understand both the differences that make understanding difficult between groups and nations, and the shared human needs and interests that make understanding essential if common problems are to be solved.

The task of teaching intelligent world citizenship seems so vast that it is tempting to throw one's hands up and say that it cannot be done, and that we had better stick with our own nation. Even understanding our own nation, of course, requires a study of its component groups, and this was rarely done in the United States in previous eras. It also requires understanding immigration and its history, which would lead the mind naturally to the problems elsewhere that give rise to immigration. Nor should one grant that there is any way of adequately understanding one's own nation and its history without setting that history in a global context. All good historical study of one's own nation requires some grounding in world history. Today, however, we need world history and global understanding for reasons that go beyond what is required to understand our own nation. The problems we face and the responsibilities we bear call on us to study the nations and cultures of the world in a more focused and systematic way.

Think, for example, of what it takes to understand the origins of the products we use in our daily lives: our soft drinks, our clothing, our coffee, our food. In earlier eras, educators who focused on democratic citizenship insisted on taking children through the complicated story of the labor that produced such products—as a lesson in the way their own nation had constructed its economy and its menu of jobs, rewards, and opportunities. This type of understanding was and is important for citizenship, since it prompts awareness of and concern for the different groups that make up our society, their different work and living conditions. Today, however, any such story is of necessity a world story. We cannot understand where even a simple soft drink comes from without thinking about lives in other nations. When we do so, it makes sense to ask about the working conditions of these people, their education, their labor relations. And when we ask such questions we need to think about our responsibilities to these people, as agents in the creation of their daily circumstances. How has the international network of which we consumers are a crucial part shaped their labor conditions? What opportunities do they have? Should we agree to be part of the causal network that produces their situation, or should we demand changes? How might we promote a decent living standard for those outside our borders who produce what we need—just as we usually feel ourselves committed to doing for workers within our borders?

To think about these questions well, young people need to understand how the global economy works. They also need to understand the history of such arrangements—the role of colonialism in the past, of foreign investment and multinational corporations more recently—so that they see how arrangements that in many cases were not chosen by local inhabitants determine their life opportunities.

Equally crucial to the success of democracies in our world is the understanding of the world's many religious traditions. There is no area (except, perhaps, sexuality) where people are more likely to form demeaning stereotypes of the other that impede mutual respect and productive discussion. Children are naturally curious about the rituals, ceremonies, and celebrations of other nations and religions, so it is a good idea to capitalize on this curiosity early, presenting stories of the world's varied traditions in an age-appropriate form, asking children from different backgrounds to describe their own beliefs and practices, and, in general, creating in the classroom a sense of global curiosity and respect. Children can just as well hear a Hindu or Buddhist story sometimes, and not always a classic American story expressing Protestant American values. (In fact, Hinduism and Buddhism are the most rapidly growing religions in the United States, so exposure of this sort will foster not just better global citizenship but better U.S. citizenship as well.) Curricula should be carefully planned from an early age to impart an ever richer and more nuanced knowledge of the world, its histories and cultures.

Our historical examples shed light on this goal as well. Returning to Tagore's school in India, let us ask how he set out to form responsible citizens of a pluralistic nation in a complex interlocking world. Tagore was preoccupied throughout his life with the problem of ethnic and religious conflict and with the need for international cooperation. In *Nationalism* he argues that India's most urgent challenge is to overcome divisions of caste and religion and the unjust, humiliating treatment of people because of their caste and religion. In *The Religion of Man* he extends his analysis to the world stage, arguing that the nations of the world are now face-to-face, and can only avoid cataclysm if they learn to understand one another and to pursue, cooperatively, the future of humanity as a whole. Tagore believed that the horrors of World War I were caused in large part by cultural failings, as nations taught their young people to prefer domination to mutual understanding and reciprocity. He set out to create a school that would do better, forming people who would be capable of cooperative, respectful international discussion.

Accordingly, Tagore's school developed strategies to make students global citizens, able to think responsibly about the future of humanity as a whole. A crucial starting point was to educate children, from an early age, about different religious and ethnic traditions. Festivals celebrated friendship among Hindus, Christians, and Muslims,[1] and children often learned about other customs through enacting festivals in the different religions.[2] Always the effort was to root the student's education in the local, giving each a firm grasp of Bengali language and traditions, and then to expand their horizons to embrace the more distant.

Visva-Bharati, the university founded by Tagore to extend his plan of liberal arts education to the university level, took the idea of world citizenship yet further, thinking of education as aspiring to a nuanced interdisciplinary type of global citizenship and understanding. A 1929 prospectus states:

> College students are expected to become familiar with the working of existing institutions and new movements inaugurated in the different countries of the world for the amelioration of the social condition of the masses. They are also required to undertake a study of interna-

tional organizations so that their outlook may become better adjusted to the needs of peace.[3]

This is but a partial description of the envisaged education, but it indicates that Tagore's goals had a lot in common with what I am recommending, although my proposals focus somewhat more than his on the need for factually accurate historical information and technical economic understanding.

Dewey also aimed education at global citizenship, from the earliest days of the child's schooling. Dewey always emphasized that history and geography should be taught in ways that promoted an adequate confrontation with the practical problems of the present. Economic history was a crucial part of what students needed to learn. Dewey believed that when history was taught with an exclusive focus on political and military aspects, democratic citizenship suffered: "Economic history is more human, more democratic, and hence more liberalizing than political history. It deals not with the rise and fall of principalities and powers, but with the growth of the effective liberties, through command of nature, of the common man for whom powers and principalities exist.[4] This statement seems relatively unsurprising today, since—whatever goes on in elementary school classrooms—most professional historians acknowledge the great importance of economic and social history, and the field has produced a large amount of excellent work concerning daily life and economic interaction. At the time, however, Dewey's was a radical statement, since both instruction and scholarship were preoccupied with "powers and principalities."

Dewey practiced what he preached. In his Laboratory School, for example, even very young children would learn to ask about the processes that produced the things they were using every day.

Weaving cloth, they would learn where the materials came from, how they were made, and what chain of labor and exchange led to the materials being there in the classroom. Typically this process would lead them far from home, not only into regions of their own country about which they previously knew little, but also into many other nations. Children also took care of animals and a garden, learning in that way what it was really like to care for such things on a daily basis, something that Dewey found more valuable than any number of artificial "object lessons" presented in the classroom, and something that also led to curiosity about forms of cultivation and care in other parts of the world. In general, as we have already seen, children learned to see their daily lives as continuous with what they learned in school, and to take from school something meaningful that they could employ in their daily lives. Dewey emphasized that such a focus on real-life activity is pedagogically useful as well; children are more lively, more focused, than when they are mere passive recipients. "[T]he great thing," he concluded, ". . . is that each shall have the education which enables him to see within his daily work all there is in it of large and human significance."[5]

We can see from this passage that Dewey is misunderstood if he is read as denigrating the humanities and suggesting that all learning has to be useful as a mere instrument to some immediate practical end. What Dewey (like Rousseau) disliked was abstract learning uncoupled from human life. His conception of human life, however, was a capacious and nonreductive one, which insisted on human relationships rich in meaning, emotion, and curiosity.

Education for global citizenship is a vast and complex subject that needs to involve the contributions of history, geography, the interdisciplinary study of culture, the history of law and political systems, and the study of religion—all interacting with one another, and all operating in increasingly sophisticated ways as children mature. And such education is also complex in its pedagogical demands. Dewey and Tagore rightly emphasized the importance of active learning for young children. As children grow older, although the connection to real life and activity should never be lost, understanding can become more theoretically sophisticated. There is no single prescription for how to do this, and many good ways in which it can be done. We can at least, however, describe some bad ways.

One bad way was the norm when I was in school: simply not to learn anything about Asia or Africa, their history and cultures, and not to learn anything about the major religions of the world, other than Christianity and Judaism. We did learn a little something about Latin America, but on the whole our eyes were fixed on Europe and North America. This means that we never saw the world as a world, never understood the dynamics of interaction among its component nations and peoples, never understood, even, how the products we use every day were produced, or where. How, then, could we ever think responsibly about public policy toward other nations, about trade relations, about the host of issues (from environment to human rights) that need to be confronted cooperatively in a way that transcends national boundaries?

Another bad way of teaching world history is that chosen by the Hindu Right in India, in the set of history and social studies textbooks they introduced during their brief ascendancy. These books did address the whole world—in a way. But they interpreted world history in the light of an ideology of Hindu supremacy.

Hindus are portrayed as a superior civilization, among the civilizations of the world. When they lived unmixed with other peoples, their society was an ideal one. Muslims, by contrast, are always portrayed as warlike and aggressive, trouble in the Indian subcontinent beginning with their advent. Moreover, so the books related, Hindus are indigenous to the land, whereas other ethnic and religious groups are foreigners. This is a myth, for the ancestors of India's Hindus almost certainly migrated into the subcontinent from outside, as both historical linguistics and the history of material culture demonstrate.[6] Global understanding is never advanced by lies, and yet the whole history of the world and its varied cultures was portrayed through this distorting lens.

These were errors of commission. Equally serious were errors of omission: the books' utter failure to portray differences of caste, class, and gender as sources of social disadvantage in early India, thus suggesting, wrongly, that early India was a glorious place of equality, where nobody was subordinated. The critical spirit that needs to inform all education for world citizenship was totally suppressed.

Finally, the books were pedagogically terrible. They failed to teach students how historical narratives are built up from evidence, and they taught no skills of sifting and evaluating evidence. Instead, they encouraged rote memorization, discouraged critical thinking, and suggested that there is simply one obvious right story (of Hindu glory and perfection) that no respectable person could challenge.[7]

As this bad example, and the good examples of FPSPI and Model UN, show us, world history, geography, and cultural study will promote human development only if they are taught in a way that is infused by searching, critical thinking. (The Model UN is a terrific way of encouraging this sort of learning, as is Future Problem Solving Program International, a multinational program in which children learn to design solutions to global problems using critical thinking and imagination.)[8] Even if the correct facts are presented to students, as was not the case here, history cannot be taught well if it is taught as a parade of facts, an all too common approach. Good teaching requires teaching children to see how history is put together from sources and evidence of many kinds, to learn to evaluate evidence, and to learn how to evaluate one historical narrative against another. Criticism also enters into classroom discussion about what has been learned; when a culture's history and economy are studied, questions should be raised about differences of power and opportunity, about the place of women and minorities, about the merits and disadvantages of different structures of political organization.

In curricular-content terms, the goal of world citizenship suggests that all young people should learn the rudiments of world history (with a focus on social and economic as well as political history), with increasing sophistication as time goes on, and should get a rich and nonstereotyped understanding of the major world religions.

At the same time, they should also learn how to "specialize"— how, that is, they might inquire in more depth into at least one unfamiliar tradition—in this way acquiring tools that can later be used elsewhere. In school this is often done well by allowing students to do research on some particular country. Despite all the defects of my own earlier education, my school was alert to the value of specialized research; in the fifth and sixth grades I was assigned reports on Uruguay and Austria, and I still remember a good deal more about these countries than what I learned in general about South America and Europe. We were even required to study the economies of these nations and their trade relations, though this study was limited to learning major exports and imports and domestic products.

There is no doubt that young children can begin to understand the principles of economics. Dewey had great success getting children to think searchingly about the origins of common products that they used and the mechanisms of exchange governing people's access to them. As children grow older, this knowledge can be made more complex, until at the end of high school children have a grasp of enough about the workings of the global economy to make informed decisions as consumers and voters.

A neglected aspect of learning for world citizenship is foreign language instruction. All students should learn at least one foreign language well. Seeing how another group of intelligent human beings has cut up the world differently, how all translation is imperfect interpretation, gives a young person an essential lesson in cultural humility. European schools on the whole perform this task very well, aware that children will actually need to become fluent in some other language (usually English). Schools in India also do pretty well in this area, in the sense that many children become fluent in English, in addition to learning their own mother tongue, and many of those whose mother tongue is not one of the widely used Indian languages (such as Hindi, Bengali, and Tamil) will often learn one of those in addition. Americans, by contrast, are complacent, used to thinking that English is all they will ever need to know. Our schools therefore begin foreign language learning much too late in most cases, missing the window of opportunity when language is most easily mastered and deeply internalized. Even if the language learned is that of a relatively familiar culture, the understanding of difference that a foreign language conveys is irreplaceable.

I have spoken of the study of other countries: What of one's own? Students should still spend a disproportionate amount of time on their own nation and its history, but they should do so as citizens of the world, meaning people who see their own nation as part of a complex interlocking world, in economic, political, and cultural relationships with other nations and peoples. Where the nation itself is concerned, they should be encouraged to be curious about the different groups that compose it and their varied histories and differential life opportunities. An adequate education for living in a pluralistic democracy must be multicultural, by which I mean one that acquaints students with some fundamentals about the histories and cultures of the many different groups with whom they share laws and institutions. These should include religious, ethnic, economic, social, and gender-based groups. Language learning, history, economics, and political science all play a role in facilitating this understanding—in different ways at different levels.

When students reach college or university, they need to develop their capacities as citizens of the world with greater sophistication. As with critical thinking, citizen-of-the-world education should form part of the basic liberal arts portion of the curriculum, whether the student's focus is business, or engineering, or philosophy, or physics. At this point, history courses can become more searching and complex, and the focus on historical method and the assessment of evidence more explicit. Similarly, courses on comparative religion can become more sophisticated and historically comprehensive.

Also, at this time, all students should acquire a solid understanding of the basic principles of economics and the operations of the global economy, building on earlier grounding. The usual introductory economics course is likely to be a bit insular, detaching principles and methods from a study of alternative economic theories and of globalization, but such courses do at least convey mastery of core techniques and principles. They can be usefully supplemented with a course on globalization and human values, taught from the point of view of both history and political theory. At the same time, all of the ideas involved in the history studied can be appreciated at a deeper level through a course in theories of social and global justice, taught from the point of view of philosophy and political theory. Students who have been lucky enough to have Socratic training in school will be especially well placed to embark on such a philosophy course. But if students get the education I am recommending here, they will all be studying philosophy at the college level as well, so they will be able to enter a more advanced course on justice with a solid preparation.

At the college level the need to "specialize" becomes all the more obvious, since a lot of what students need to learn about an unfamiliar culture requires in-depth familiarity with its history and traditions. Only then can they appreciate how differences of class, caste, and religion create different life opportunities; how urban lives differ from rural lives; how different forms of political organization lead to different human opportunities; how even the family organization and the roles of women and men can be subtly altered by public policies and laws. No student could be expected to learn all this about all the major countries of the world, so an in-depth focus on one unfamiliar tradition is essential. Once students learn how to inquire, and what questions to ask, they can transfer their learning to another part of the world (with which they might be dealing in their work).

Colleges cannot convey the type of learning that produces global citizens unless they have a liberal arts structure: that is, a set of general education courses for all students outside the requirements of the major subject. Nations that, like India, lack this structure can try to convey the same learning in secondary school, but this is really not sufficient for responsible citizenship. The more sophisticated learning that can only be done at a later age is indispensable in forming citizens who have real understanding of global issues and accountability for the policy choices made by their own nation. The need for liberal arts courses is being increasingly recognized in nations that do not have this structure. In India, for example, the highly prestigious Institutes of Technology and Management (IITs) have been in the vanguard of introducing humanities courses for all their participants. One professor at IIT-Mumbai told me that they regard these courses as playing a crucial function in promoting respectful interactions among students from different religious and caste backgrounds, as well as preparing them for a society in which such differences must be respectfully confronted.[9]

Does global citizenship really require the humanities? It requires a lot of factual knowledge, and students might get this without a humanistic education—for example, from absorbing the facts in standardized textbooks such as those used by the BJP, only with correct rather than incorrect facts, and by learning the basic techniques of economics. Responsible citizenship requires, however, a lot more: the ability to assess historical evidence, to use and think critically about economic principles, to assess accounts of social justice, to speak a foreign language, to appreciate the complexities of the major world religions. The factual part alone could be purveyed without the skills and techniques we have come to associate with the humanities. But a catalogue of facts, without the ability to assess them, or to understand how a narrative is assembled from evidence, is almost as bad as ignorance, since the pupil will not be able to distinguish ignorant stereotypes purveyed by politicians and cultural leaders from the truth, or bogus claims from valid ones. World history and economic understanding, then, must be humanistic and critical if they are to be at all useful in forming intelligent global citizens, and they must be taught alongside the study of religion and of philosophical theories of justice. Only then will they supply a useful foundation for the public debates that we must have if we are to cooperate in solving major human problems.

VI

Cultivating Imagination: Literature and the Arts

We may become powerful by knowledge, but we attain fullness by sympathy. . . . But we find that this education of sympathy is not only systematically ignored in schools, but it is
severely repressed.
— Rabindranath Tagore, "My School," 1916

It will be observed that I am looking at the highly sophisticated adult's enjoyment of living or of beauty or of abstract
human contrivance, and at the same time at the creative gesture of a baby who reaches out for the mother's mouth and
feels her teeth, and at the same time looks into her eyes, seeing her creatively. For me, playing leads on naturally to cultural experience and indeed forms its foundation.
— Donald Winnicott, *Playing and Reality*, 1971

Citizens cannot relate well to the complex world around them by
factual knowledge and logic alone. The third ability of the citizen,
closely related to the first two, is what we can call the narrative
imagination.[1] This means the ability to think what it might be

like to be in the shoes of a person different from oneself, to be an intelligent reader of that person's story, and to understand the emotions and wishes and desires that someone so placed might have. The cultivation of sympathy has been a key part of the best modern ideas of democratic education, in both Western and non-Western nations. Much of this cultivation must take place in the family, but schools, and even colleges and universities, also play an important role. If they are to play it well, they must give a central role in the curriculum to the humanities and the arts, cultivating a participatory type of education that activates and refines the capacity to see the world through another person's eyes.

Children, I have said, are born with a rudimentary capacity for sympathy and concern. Their earliest experiences, however, are typically dominated by a powerful narcissism, as anxiety about nourishment and comfort are still unlinked to any secure grasp of the reality of others. Learning to see another human being not as a thing but as a full person is not an automatic event but an achievement that requires overcoming many obstacles, the first of which is the sheer inability to distinguish between self and other. Fairly early in the typical experience of a human infant, this distinction gradually becomes evident, as babies sort out by coordination of tactile and visual sensations the fact that some of the things they see are parts of their own bodies and others are not. But a child may grasp that its parents are not parts of itself, without at all grasping that they have an inner world of thought and feeling, and without granting that this inner world makes demands on the child's own conduct. It is easy for narcissism to take charge at this point, casting others as mere instruments of the child's own wishes and feelings.

The capacity for genuine concern for others has several preconditions. One, as Rousseau emphasized, is a degree of practical competence: a child who knows how to do things for herself does not need to make others her slaves, and growing physical maturity usually frees children from total narcissistic dependence on others. A second precondition, which I have emphasized in talking about disgust and shame, is a recognition that total control is neither possible nor good, that the world is a place in which we all have weaknesses and need to find ways to support one another. This recognition involves the ability to see the world as a place in which one is not alone—a place in which other people have their own lives and needs, and entitlements to pursue those needs. But my second precondition constitutes a complex achievement. How would one ever come to see the world this way, from having seen it as a place where other shapes move around ministering to one's own demands?

Part of the answer to this question is no doubt given in our innate equipment. The natural interplay of smiles between baby and parent shows a readiness to recognize humanity in another, and babies quickly take delight in those recognitions. Another part of the answer, however, is given by play, which supplies a crucial third precondition of concern: the ability to imagine what the experience of another might be like.

One of the most influential and attractive accounts of imaginative play is that of Donald Winnicott (1896–1971), the British pediatrician and psychoanalyst. Winnicott began practicing psychoanalysis after many years of treating a wide range of children in his pediatric practice, which he continued throughout his life. His views are thus informed by a wider range of clinical experiences than are those of most psychoanalytic thinkers, a fact that he often emphasized, saying that he was not interested in curing symptoms, but in dealing with whole people, living and loving. Whatever their origin, his views about play in children's development have had a large and widespread cultural influence that does not depend on any prior sympathy with psychoanalytic ideas. (For example, it seems likely, as Winnicott himself believed, that Linus's security blanket in Charles Schultz's *Peanuts* cartoons is a representation of Winnicott's idea of the "transitional object.")

As a doctor who observed many healthy children, Winnicott had confidence in the unfolding of the developmental process, which would produce ethical concern—and the basis for a healthy democracy—as an outgrowth of early struggles, if things went well enough. He felt that development usually goes well, and that parents usually do a good job. Parents are preoccupied with their infants early on, and attend to their needs well, enabling the child's self to develop gradually and eventually express itself. (Winnicott typically used the word "mother," but he always emphasized that "mother" was a functional category, and that the role could be played by parents of either or both sexes. He also emphasized the maternal nature of his own role as analyst.)

At first the infant cannot grasp the parent as a definite object, and thus cannot have full-fledged emotions. Its world is symbiotic and basically narcissistic. Gradually, however, infants develop the capacity to be alone—aided by their "transitional objects," the name Winnicott gave to the blankets and stuffed animals that enable children to comfort themselves when the parent is absent. Eventually the child usually develops the ability to "play alone in the presence of its mother," a key sign of growing confidence in the developing self. At this point, the child begins to be able to relate to the parent as a whole person rather than as an extension of its own needs.

Play, Winnicott believed, is crucial to this entire phase of development. Having been raised in a repressive ultra-religious household in which imaginative play was strongly discouraged, and having experienced serious relational difficulties in adult life as a result, he came to believe that play was a key to healthy personality growth.[2] Play is a type of activity that takes place in the space between people—what Winnicott calls a "potential space." Here people (children first, adults later) experiment with the idea of otherness in ways that are less threatening than the direct encounter with another may often be.[3] They thus get invaluable practice in empathy and reciprocity. Play begins in magical fantasies in which the child controls what happens—as with the self-comforting games that a young child may play with its "transitional object." But as confidence and trust develop in interpersonal play with the parents or with other children, control is relaxed and the child is able to experiment with vulnerability and surprise in ways that could be distressing outside the play setting, but are delightful in play. Think, for example, of the tireless delight with which small children play at the disappearance and reappearance of a parent, or a cherished object.

As play develops, the child develops a capacity for wonder. Simple nursery rhymes already urge children to put themselves in the place of a small animal, another child, even an inanimate object. "Twinkle, twinkle, little star, how I wonder what you are," is a paradigm of wonder, since it involves looking at a shape and endowing that shape with an inner world. That is what children ultimately must be able to do with other people. Nursery rhymes and stories are thus a crucial preparation for concern in life.[4] The presence of the other, which can be very threatening, becomes, in play, a delightful source of curiosity, and this curiosity contributes toward the development of healthy attitudes in friendship, love, and, later, political life.

Winnicott understood that the "potential space" between people does not close up just because they become adults. Life is full of occasions for wonder and play, and he emphasized that sexual relations, and intimacy generally, are areas in which the capacity for play is crucial. People can close up, forgetting the inner world of others, or they can retain and further develop the capacity to endow the forms of others, in imagination, with inner life. Everyone who knew Winnicott was struck by his unusual capacity to connect with others through play and empathy. With patients, particularly child patients, he had a tireless ability to enter the world of the child's games and cherished objects, their stuffed animals, their fantasies about a sibling's birth. But play, for him, did not cease where the "adult world" began. His adult patients, too, praised his capacity for taking the position of the other. Sixty-year-old analyst Harry Guntrip described this gift in a journal of his analysis with Winnicott: "I could let my tension go and develop and relax because you were present in my inner world." Play was also a feature of Winnicott's non-therapeutic relationships. He and his wife were famous for their elaborate jokes and pranks; his papers contain silly drawings and poems they wrote to each other during boring meetings.[5]

Winnicott often emphasized that play has an important role in shaping democratic citizenship. Democratic equality brings vulnerability. As one of his patients perceptively remarked, "The alarming thing about equality is that we are then both children and the question is, where is father? We know where we are if one of us is the father."[6] Play teaches people to be capable of living with others without control; it connects the experiences of vulnerability and surprise to curiosity and wonder, rather than to crippling anxiety.

How do adults sustain and develop their capacity for play after they have left behind the world of children's games? Winnicott argued that a key role is played by the arts. He held that a primary function of art in all human cultures is to preserve and enhance the cultivation of the "play space," and he saw the role of the arts in human life as, above all, that of nourishing and extending the capacity for empathy. In the sophisticated response to a complex work of art, he saw a continuation of the baby's delight in games and role-playing.

The earlier progressive educators, whose views we described in chapter 4, though unacquainted with Winnicott's writings, understood from their own reflection and experience his basic insight that play is crucial to the development of a healthy personality. They found fault with traditional schools for not comprehending the educational value of play, and they insisted that play be incorporated into the structure of education, both early and late. Froebel focused on the need of very young children to explore their environment through manipulating objects and using their imaginations to endow simple shapes (the sphere, the cube) with stories and personalities. Pestalozzi's fictional heroine Gertrude saw that passive rote learning deadened the personality, whereas practical activities, carried on in a playful spirit, enriched the personality.

Such educators realized early on that the most important contribution of the arts to life after school was that of strengthening the personality's emotional and imaginative resources, giving children abilities to understand both self and others that they would otherwise lack. We do not automatically see another human being as spacious and deep, having thoughts, spiritual longings, and emotions. It is all too easy to see another person as just a body—which we might then think we can use for our ends, bad or good. It is an achievement to see a soul in that body, and this achievement is supported by poetry and the arts, which ask us to wonder about the inner world of that shape we see—and, too, to wonder about ourselves and our own depths.

Technical and factual education can easily lack this cultivation. Philosopher John Stuart Mill (1806–1873), as a precocious child, received a superb education in languages, history, and the sciences, but this education did not cultivate his emotional or imaginative resources. As a young adult, he suffered a crippling depression. He credited his eventual recovery to the influence of Wordsworth's poetry, which educated his emotions and made it possible for him to look for emotion in others. In later life, Mill developed an account of what he called the "religion of humanity" based on the cultivation of sympathy he had found through his experience of poetry.

At around the same time, in America, Bronson Alcott, whose Socratic pedagogy in the Temple School we studied in chapter 4, gave the same idea of poetic education a curricular shape. Drawing on Wordsworth, and using his poems often in the classroom, he held that poetry cultivates a child's inner space, nourishing both imaginative and emotional capacities. In Louisa Alcott's *Little Men*, the imaginative games played at Plumtree School are just as important as the intellectual lessons, and are interwoven with them. Both lessons and games, in turn, are enlivened with a spirit of loving reciprocity, as the school, run like a large family, remarkably anticipates Winnicott's idea that sophisticated artistic play is a continuation of the play between parents and child.

The most elaborate development of the arts as a linchpin of early education, however, awaited the twentieth century and the theoretically sophisticated school experiments of Tagore in India and Dewey in the United States. Dewey wrote a good deal about the arts as key ingredients in a democratic society, and it is clear even today that the cultivation of imagination through music and theater plays a key role in the Laboratory School. Dewey insisted that what is of importance for children is not "fine art," meaning some contemplative exercise in which children learn to "appreciate" works of art as things cut off from the real world. Nor should children be taught to believe that imagination is pertinent only in the domain of the unreal or imaginary. Instead, they need to see an imaginative dimension in all their interactions, and to see works of art as just one domain in which imagination is cultivated. "[T]he difference between play and what is regarded as serious employment should be not a difference between the presence and absence of imagination, but a difference in the materials with which imagination is occupied." In a successful school, children will come to see that imagination is required to deal with anything that lies "beyond the scope of direct physical response."[7] And this would include pretty much everything that matters: a conversation with a friend, a study of economic transactions, a scientific experiment.

Let me focus here, however, on Tagore's use of the arts, since his school was the school of an artist, and one that gave music, theater, poetry, painting, and dance all a central role from the very start of a child's enrollment. In chapter 4 we studied Tagore's commitment to Socratic questioning. But Socratic inquiry can appear cold and unemotional, and the relentless pursuit of logical argument can risk stunting other parts of the personality, a danger that Tagore foresaw and determined to avoid. For him, the primary role played by the arts was the cultivation of sympathy, and he noted that this role for education—perhaps one of its most important roles—had been "systematically ignored" and "severely repressed" by standard models of education. The arts, in his view, promote both inner self-cultivation and responsiveness to others. The two typically develop in tandem, since one can hardly cherish in another what one has not explored in oneself.

As we have mentioned, Tagore used role-playing throughout the school day, as intellectual positions were explored by asking children to take up unfamiliar postures of thought. This role-playing, we can now add, was no mere logical game. It was a way of cultivating sympathy hand in hand with the cultivation of the logical faculties. He also used role-playing to explore the difficult area of religious difference, as students were urged to celebrate the rituals and ceremonies of religions not their own, understanding the unfamiliar through imaginative participation. Above all, though, Tagore used elaborate theatrical productions, mingling drama, music, and dance, to get children to explore different roles with the full participation of their bodies, taking up unfamiliar stances and gestures. Dance was a key part of the school for both boys and girls, since Tagore understood that exploration of the unfamiliar requires the willingness to put aside bodily stiffness and shame in order to inhabit a role.

Women were his particular concern, since he saw that women were typically brought up to be ashamed of their bodies and unable to move freely, particularly in the presence of men. A lifelong advocate of women's freedom and equality, he saw that simply telling girls to move more freely would be unlikely to overcome years of repression, but giving them precisely choreographed moves to perform, leaping from here to there, would be a more successful incentive to freedom. (Tagore's sister-in-law invented the blouse that is ubiquitously worn, today, with the sari, since he asked her to devise something that would allow women to move freely without fearing that their sari would expose their bodies in an inappropriate way.) At the same time, men too explored challenging roles in dance, under the aegis of Tagore, a great dancer as well as a famous choreographer, and known for his sinuous and androgynous movements. Explicit themes of gender equality were common in the dramas, as in *Land of Cards*, described in chapter 4, in which women take the lead in rejecting ossified traditions.

Amita Sen, the mother of Nobel Prize–winning Amartya Sen, was a pupil in the school from her earliest childhood days, since her father, a well-known expert on the history of the Hindu religion, went there to teach shortly after the school's founding. A small child playing in the garden near Tagore's window, she inspired his well-known poem "Chota mai," in which he describes how a little girl disturbed his work. Later, as a young bride, she inspired another well-known Tagore poem, about a young woman "stepping into the waters of life, unafraid." In between, she was a pupil in the school, and she proved to be one of its most talented dancers, so she took on leading roles in those dance dramas. Later, she wrote two books about the school; one, *Joy in All Work*, has been translated into English, and it describes Tagore's activity as dancer and choreographer.[8]

Amita Sen understood that the purpose of Tagore's dance dramas was not just the production of some fine artworks, but also the cultivation of emotion and imagination in his pupils. Her detailed account of the role of theater and dance in the school shows how all the "regular" education in Santiniketan, the education hat enabled these students to perform well in standard examinations, was infused with passion, creativity, and delight because of the way in which education was combined with dance and song.

> His dance was a dance of emotion. The playful clouds in the sky, the shivering of the wind in the leaves, light glistening on the grass, moonlight flooding the earth, the blossoming and fading of flowers, the murmur of dry leaves—the pulsing of joy in a man's heart, or the pangs of sorrow, are all expressed in this expressive dance's movements and expressions.[9]

We should bear in mind that we hear the voice of an older woman recalling her childhood experience. How extraordinary that the emotions and the poetry of the child live on so vigorously in the woman, and what a tribute this is to the capacity of this sort of education for a kind of enlivening of the personality that continues on in one's life when all learned facts are forgotten. Of course, as her book makes clear, this could not be done by simply leaving children on their own to play around; instruction in the arts requires discipline and ambition, if it is to stretch and extend the capacities for both empathy and expression.

Instruction in literature and the arts can cultivate sympathy in many ways, through engagement with many different works of literature, music, fine art, and dance. Tagore was ahead of the West in his focus on music and dance, which we in the United States cultivate only intermittently. But thought needs to be given to what the student's particular blind spots are likely to be, and texts should be chosen in consequence. For all societies at all times have their particular blind spots, groups within their culture and also groups abroad that are especially likely to be dealt with ignorantly and obtusely. Works of art (whether literary or musical or theatrical) can be chosen to promote criticism of this obtuseness, and a more adequate vision of the unseen. Ralph Ellison, in a later essay about his great novel *Invisible Man*, wrote that a novel such as his could be "a raft of perception, hope, and entertainment" on which American culture could "negotiate the snags and whirlpools" that stand between us and our democratic ideal.[10] His novel, of course, takes the "inner eyes" of the white reader as its theme and its target. The hero is invisible to white society, but he tells us that this invisibility is an imaginative and educational failing on the part of white people, not a biological accident on his. Through the imagination, Ellison suggests, we are able to develop our ability to see the full humanness of the people with whom our encounters in daily life are especially likely to be superficial at best, at worst infected by demeaning stereotypes. And stereotypes usually abound when our world has constructed sharp separations between groups, and suspicions that make any encounter difficult.

In Ellison's America, the central challenge for the "inner eyes" was that of race, a stigmatized position almost impossible for the conventional white reader to inhabit. For Tagore, as we have seen, a particular cultural blind spot was the agency and intelligence of women, and he ingeniously devised ways to promote a fuller curiosity and respect between the sexes. Both writers claim that information about social stigma and inequality will not convey the full understanding a democratic citizen needs without a participatory experience of the stigmatized position, which theater and literature both enable. The reflections of Tagore and Ellison suggest that schools that omit the arts omit essential occasions for democratic understanding. An Indian acquaintance of mine expressed frustration that as a child in Indian government schools he never got the chance to explore different social positions through theater, whereas his nieces and nephews in the United States learned about the civil rights movement in part by putting on a play about Rosa Parks in which the experience of sitting in the back of the bus conveyed information about stigma that could not have been fully conveyed without that participatory experience.

So we need to cultivate students' "inner eyes," and this means carefully crafted instruction in the arts and humanities—appropriate to the child's age and developmental level—that will bring students in contact with issues of gender, race, ethnicity, and cross-cultural experience and understanding. This artistic instruction can and should be linked to the citizen-of-the-world instruction, since works of art are frequently an invaluable way of beginning to understand the achievements and sufferings of a culture different from one's own.

In other words, the role of the arts in schools and colleges is twofold. They cultivate capacities for play and empathy in a general way, and they address particular cultural blind spots. The first role can be played by works remote from the student's own time and place, although not just any randomly selected work. The second requires a more pointed focus on areas of social unease. The two roles are in some ways continuous, since the general capacity, once developed, makes it far easier to address a stubborn blind spot.

Both, in order to be stably linked to democratic values, require a normative view about how human beings ought to relate to one another (as equals, as dignified, as having inner depth and worth), and both therefore require selectivity regarding the artworks used. The empathetic imagination can be capricious and uneven if not linked to an idea of equal human dignity. It is all too easy to have refined sympathy for those close to us in geography, or class, or race, and to refuse it to people at a distance, or members of minority groups, treating them as mere things. Moreover, there are plenty of artworks that reinforce uneven sympathies. Children who are asked to cultivate their imaginations by reading racist literature, or pornographic objectification of women, would not be cultivating them in a way appropriate to democratic societies, and we cannot deny that antidemocratic movements have known how to use the arts, music, and rhetoric in ways that contribute further to demeaning and stigmatizing certain groups and people.[11] The imaginative component of democratic education requires careful selectivity. What we should notice, however, is that the way these defective forms of "literature" operate is by inhibiting imaginative access to the stigmatized position—by treating minorities, or women, as mere things with no experiences worth exploring. The imaginative activity of exploring another inner life, while not the whole of a healthy moral relationship to others, is at least one necessary ingredient of it. Moreover, it contains within itself an antidote to the self-protective fear that is so often connected to egocentric projects of control. When people take up the play attitude toward others, they are less likely—at least for the time being—to see them as looming threats to their safety whom they must keep in line.

The cultivation of imagination that I have described is closely linked to the Socratic capacity for criticism of dead or inadequate traditions, and provides essential support for this critical activity. One can hardly treat another person's intellectual position respectfully unless one at least tries to see what outlook on life and what life experiences generated it. But what we have said about egoistic anxiety prepares us to see there is something further that the arts contribute to Socratic criticism. As Tagore often emphasized, the arts, by generating pleasure in connection with acts of subversion and cultural reflection, produce an enduring and even attractive dialogue with the prejudices of the past, rather than one fraught with fear and defensiveness. This is what Ellison meant by calling *Invisible Man* "a raft of perception, hope, and entertainment." Entertainment is crucial to the ability of the arts to offer perception and hope. It is not just the experience of the performer, then, that is so important for democracy, it is the way in which performance offers a venue for exploring difficult issues without crippling anxiety.

Similarly, Tagore's notorious dance performance, in which Amita Sen danced the role of the Green Fairy, was a milestone for women because it was artistically distinguished and extremely enjoyable. So was the even more daring drama in which Amita danced the role of the queen, and the text accompanying her movements was, "Come to my breast." The text ultimately had to be changed to "Come to my heart"—but, Amita told me, "Everyone knew what was really being said." That episode could have set back the cause of women, but it advanced it, because the erotic agency of the queen, beautifully danced by Amita, was delightful. In the end, the audience could not sustain habits of shock and anger, against the gentle assault of beautiful music and movement.

We have touched on images of gender, and perhaps there is nothing more essential to the health of a democracy than having healthy images of what a real man is, and how a real man relates both to women and to other men. This issue was recognized as central from the very beginning of modern democratic culture, in both Western and non-Western nations. In Europe, the philosopher Johann Gottfried Herder, writing in 1792, insisted that good citizens needed to learn that manliness does not require warlike aggressiveness against other nations. Alluding to what he understood to be the custom of Native Americans, he said that the men of Europe, similarly, should put on women's clothes when they deliberate about war and peace, and should in general cultivate a "reduced respect" for warlike exploits and a horror of a "false statecraft" that whips people up into eagerness for conquest. Instead, both men and women alike should cultivate "dispositions of peace"—in the service of which, he suggested, assuming a female role for a time might be very useful.[12]

Similar ideas were explored in India by both Tagore and Gandhi. Tagore's school, through its dance idiom and its emphasis on the arts, cultivated a male personality that was receptive, playful, and uninterested in dominating others. Tagore explicitly linked this goal to a repudiation of the sort of aggressive colonizing nationalism that he associated with European cultural values and norms of manliness. Gandhi, later, firmly linked his nonviolent approach to social change to a repudiation of the goal of domination in sexual relations. He deliberately cultivated a persona that was androgynous and maternal—not to show his followers that they must altogether abandon traditional gender distinctions, but to show them that one can be a real man without being aggressive, that a wide range of gender styles are all compatible with true manliness, so long as the accent is firmly on respect for human dignity in others and compassion for their needs.

In short, children need to learn that sympathetic receptivity is not unmanly, and that manliness does not mean not weeping, not sharing the grief of the hungry or the battered. This learning cannot be promoted by a confrontational approach that says, "Drop your old images of manliness." It can only be promoted by a culture that is receptive in both curricular content and pedagogical style, in which, it is not too bold to say, the capacities for love and compassion infuse the entirety of the educational endeavor.

As with critical thinking, so too with the arts. We discover that they are essential for the goal of economic growth and the maintenance of a healthy business culture. Leading business educators have long understood that a developed capacity to imagine is a keystone of a healthy business culture.[13] Innovation requires minds that are flexible, open, and creative; literature and the arts cultivate these capacities. When they are lacking, a business culture quickly loses steam. Again and again, liberal arts graduates are hired in preference to students who have had a narrower preprofessional education, precisely because they are believed to have the flexibility and the creativity to succeed in a dynamic business environment. If our only concern were national economic growth, then we should still protect humanistic liberal arts education. Today, however, as we'll see in the next chapter, the arts are under assault in schools all over the world.

At this point, a case study will help us see how crucial the arts can be in supplying ingredients for democratic citizenship in an American culture divided by both ethnicity and class. Consider the case of the Chicago Children's Choir. Chicago, like most large American cities, contains huge economic inequalities, which translate into large differences in basic housing, employment opportunities, and educational quality. Children in African American and Latino neighborhoods, in particular, are usually not getting anywhere near as good an education as children in suburban white neighborhoods, or in urban private schools. Such children may already have disadvantages in their homes—only one parent, or even no parents living with them, and no "role models" of career success, discipline, aspiration, or committed political engagement. Schools are not racially segregated by law, of course, but they are largely segregated de facto, so students are likely to have few friends from classes and races different from their own.

To make things worse, the arts, which can bring children together in nonhierarchical ways, have been severely cut back in the public schools, as part of cost-cutting measures. Into this void has stepped the Chicago Children's Choir, an organization currently supported by private philanthropy, which by now includes almost three thousand children, approximately 80 percent of whom are below the poverty line, in programs of choral singing with rigorous standards of excellence. The program has three tiers. First, there are programs in the schools; many of these take the place of programs run by the city that had been cut away. The in-school programs serve some twenty-five hundred children in more than sixty different choirs in fifty elementary schools, focusing on grades three through eight. The in-school program, as the official description of the program states, "validates the idea that music is as important as math and science to the development of the mind and the spirit."

The second tier consists of the neighborhood choirs, eight choirs in different regions of Chicago. These are after-school programs requiring auditions and some level of serious commitment, serving children from age eight to age sixteen. These children perform many times each year and tour to different parts of the country;

they learn a wide variety of music from different countries of the world and develop their musical skills.

Finally, the most advanced level, the Concert Choir, probably the top youth ensemble in the United States, has recorded numerous CDs, toured internationally, and performed with symphony orchestras and opera companies. This group performs works ranging from Bach motets to African American spirituals; the repertoire deliberately includes music from many different world cultures.

This choir system was inaugurated in 1956 by Christopher Moore, a Unitarian minister, who believed that he could change young people's lives by bringing them together through music— across differences of race, religion, and economic class. The system has grown from an initial twenty-four singers to its current size through the dedicated support of many Chicago-area donors; the city gives it free office space but makes no further financial contribution.

Such facts are easy to narrate. What is difficult to describe is the emotional impact of hearing these young people, who do not sing like the church choirs of my youth, motionless with music held in front of them. They memorize everything they sing, and sing everything expressively, at times using gesture and even dance movements to put a song across. Their faces express tremendous joy in the act of singing, and this emotion is a large part of what the program cultivates, in both performers and spectators.

I have observed rehearsals of the neighborhood Hyde Park choir, as well as public performances by the Concert Choir, and even in the highly inclusive activity of the former, one finds immense pride, musical aspiration, and personal commitment. Singers from the Concert Choir typically become mentors to the younger children, giving them role models of discipline and aspiration, and also developing their own ethos of social responsibility.

When I recently interviewed Mollie Stone, conductor of the Hyde Park neighborhood choir and associate conductor of the Concert Choir, I asked her what, in her view, the choir contributes to life in Chicago. She gave me a moving and eloquent set of answers. First, she said, the choir gives children the opportunity for an intense experience side by side with children from different racial and socioeconomic backgrounds. The experience of singing with someone, she said, includes great vulnerability; you have to blend your breath and your body with someone else's, and you have to make the sounds from within your own body, as would not be the case even with an orchestra. So, in addition, the musical experience teaches children love of their own bodies, at an age when they are likely to hate their bodies and feel very uncomfortable; they develop a sense of ability, discipline, and responsibility.

Then, since the choirs sing music from many different cultures, they learn about other cultures, and they learn that these cultures are available to them; they transcend barriers that expectation and local culture have thrown in their way, showing that they can be world citizens. By learning to sing the music of another time or place, they also find ways of showing that they respect someone else, that they are willing to spend time learning about them and taking them seriously.

In all these ways, they learn about their role in the local community and the world, and Stone emphasized that this can lead to many forms of curiosity, as choir alumni go on to study political science, history, language, visual art.

Three stories illustrate what Stone is talking about. One day, she came into the rehearsal room of the Concert Choir and heard a group of African American kids singing a complex passage of a Bach motet they had been rehearsing. "So," she said, "you're getting in some extra rehearsal today?" "No," they said. "We're just chilling. We're just jamming." The fact that these African American kids from ghetto schools felt that a natural way to "chill," to relax together, was to sing Bach, showed that they did not feel confined to "black culture"; they could claim any culture as their own and take membership in it. It was theirs as much as was the world of the African American spiritual.

Stone then remembered her own experience, when she was a young singer in a predominantly African American choir and the choir performed a Hebrew folksong. As the only Jew in the choir, she had a sudden sense of inclusion; she felt that the other kids respected her culture, took it seriously, wanted to study it and participate in it.

Finally, on a recent tour, the Hyde Park neighborhood choir went to Nashville, Tennessee, the home of country music, a place whose culture and values are somewhat alien to most northern, urban Americans—whom residents of Nashville would be likely to regard with suspicion in turn. Hearing a country music group performing outside the Grand Ole Opry, the kids recognized a country song that they had sung in choir, and they surrounded the band, joining in. A celebratory expression of inclusion and mutual respect was the result.

What the choir shows us about the role of the arts in promoting democratic inclusion and respect is not news. It is part of a long American tradition that includes the progressive educators I have mentioned (from Alcott through Dewey). Horace Mann argued that vocal music, in particular, tends to unite people of diverse backgrounds, and to reduce conflict.[14]

I have emphasized, here, the contribution the choir makes to its participants. Needless to say, this contribution is multiplied many times, through the effect on parents and families, on schools, and on audiences who hear the choir both in the United States and abroad.

Unfortunately, such enterprises are not favored by the U.S. educational establishment, local or national. The choir is therefore constantly in debt, and is able to continue to exist only through tireless volunteer donations of both time and money. Chicago is fortunate to have a number of privately funded initiatives through which major arts organizations create programs for the schools—in addition to a great deal of cost-free public art that is typically supported by public-private partnerships.

Since I have mentioned money, let's face up to this issue. The arts, it is said, are just too costly. We cannot afford them in a time of economic hardship. The arts, however, need not be expensive to promote. If people will only make room for them, they can be fostered relatively inexpensively—because children love to dance and sing, and to tell and read stories. If we think of art in the way that Dewey criticized—as highbrow "Fine Art," requiring expensive equipment and objects for its "appreciation"—we can easily be led to the conclusion that in a cost-conscious time there is not enough money for it. I have heard such arguments from educators in Chicago, and I do not buy them. I have been in rural areas of India, visiting literacy projects for women and girls that have no equipment at all—not even chairs and desks, no paper, no pens, perhaps only a slate passed from hand to hand—and there, the arts are flourishing, as young girls who are just beginning to read express themselves much more fully by putting on plays about their experiences, or singing songs of their struggles, or drawing pictures of their goals and fears. Dedicated activist teachers know that the arts are the way to get kids to come eagerly to school, to want to learn to read and write, to want to think critically about their situation in life. So often, as a visitor, I have been asked if I will teach them a song of the American women's movement—and when I volunteer "We Shall Overcome," they already know it, in every regional language. Music and dance, drawing and theater, these are powerful avenues of joy and expression for all, and it does not take much money to foster them. Indeed they are the backbone of the curriculum in rural literacy programs because they supply both children and adults with motivation to come to school, positive ways of relating to one another, and joy in the educational endeavor.

Why can't we use the arts this way in the United States? Recently I visited a program for troubled young teens at Morton Alternative, a public high school in Cicero, a city just outside of Chicago. Teens who have been kicked out of another public high school must go to Morton Alternative—unless they drop out entirely (since some are over sixteen). The school has a total of only about forty students, so individual attention is feasible. Thanks to a remarkably astute and compassionate principal, who focused on each child's history as if that child were his own son or daughter, and thanks to an arrangement with a volunteer organization of psychotherapists and social workers, all children receive a lot of individual mentoring and regular group therapy in groups of four or five. I was deeply impressed by the changes that were taking place just because some adults are listening. The school was as close to the family environment of Alcott's Plumtree School as it was possible to be when children had to return home to families that were often dysfunctional and even violent. What do you do with the arts, I asked. The principal and the head therapist seemed surprised. They had not thought of this as something helpful.

But why on earth not? These adolescents, most of them Mexican American, come from a culture with enormously rich music and dance traditions. Through these, and through theater, they could have found powerful ways to express their conflicts and aspirations. Group therapy is already a type of theater, but it does not involve the sort of disciplined achievement that putting on a play would. There was no economic reason why they were not doing this. They just had not thought about it.

Four weeks later, the head therapist sent me a poem that one of the girls in the therapy session I had observed had written as a result of his new determination to incorporate the arts into his efforts at Morton Alternative. A halting, yet extremely powerful account of her growing love for her baby, written by a teen mother who was having enormous struggles in that role, the poem did seem to me to mark a new stage in her progress toward pride and self-mastery, and the therapist supported that conclusion. It makes so much sense, and it did not cost an extra dime.

The education I recommend requires that teachers do things differently. Implementing it would require major changes in teacher training, at least in most districts in the United States and most nations of the world. It would also require most school principals (though not the principal at Morton Alternative) to change the ethos of their schools. In this sense, this education is costly. But the costs are, I believe, transition costs; there is nothing intrinsically more expensive about doing things this way. Once the new ways are in place, they will perpetuate themselves. I would even argue that a type of education that gets both students and teachers more passionately involved in thinking and imagining reduces costs by reducing the anomie and time wasting that typically accompany a lack of personal investment.

VII

Democratic Education on the Ropes

But the danger lies in this, that organised ugliness storms the mind and carries the day by its mass, by its aggressive persistence, by its power of mockery directed against the deeper sentiments of heart. . . . Therefore its rivalry with things that are modest and profound and have the subtle delicacy of life is to be dreaded.

—Tagore, *Nationalism*, 1917

And whoever walks a furlong without sympathy walks to his own funeral drest in his shroud.

—Walt Whitman, *Song of Myself*, 1855

How is education for democratic citizenship doing in the world today? Very poorly, I fear. This is a manifesto, not an empirical study, so this chapter will not be filled with quantitative data, although the data support my concern.[1] The disturbing trends I am describing must simply be summarized, and illustrated by telling and representative examples.

The argument I have been making is intended as a call to action. If it should turn out that things are less bad than I believe them to be, we should not breathe a sigh of relief; we should do exactly what we would if we believed things were pretty bleak. We should redouble our commitment to the parts of education that keep democracy vital. Even if it should turn out that they are not as profoundly threatened as I believe them to be, they are clearly vulnerable and under great pressure in an era of economic globalization.

EDUCATION OF THE TYPE I recommend is still doing reasonably well in the place where I first studied it, namely the liberal arts portion of U.S. college and university curricula. Indeed, this part of the curriculum, in institutions such as my own, still attracts generous philanthropic support, as rich people remember with pleasure the time when they read books they loved and pursued issues open-endedly. During the recent economic crisis, we have even seen an increase in commitment as donors who value the humanities dig deeper in order to preserve what they love.

It is possible to argue, indeed, that the liberal arts portion of college and university education in the United States now supports democratic citizenship better than it did fifty years ago.[2] Fifty years ago, students knew little about the world outside Europe and North America. Nor did they learn much about minorities in their own nation. History, whether world or U.S., was typically taught with an eye on large political events and dominant political actors. The story of minority or immigrant groups was rarely emphasized; nor was economic history a part of the grand narrative.

Today all this has changed for the better. New areas of study, infused into liberal arts courses for all students, have enhanced their understanding of non-Western nations, of the global economy, of race relations, of the dynamics of gender, of the history of migration and the struggles of new groups for recognition and equality. Curricula have been increasingly fashioned with an eye to good citizenship in a world of diversity, and these changes are paying off. Young people these days rarely leave college as ignorant about the non-Western world as students of my own generation routinely did.

Similar changes have taken place in the teaching of literature and the arts. Students are exposed to a far wider range of materials, and their "inner eyes" (to borrow Ellison's phrase) are cultivated by being exposed to the experiences of people of many different types, both within their own nation and abroad. The history of music is now taught with a far greater recognition of the world's many musical traditions and their interactions. Film history recognizes contributions outside the Hollywood mainstream.

We in the United States cannot be complacent about the health of the humanities, however. Despite continued support from donors, the economic crisis has led many universities to make deep cuts in humanities and arts programming. Other areas also have to make cuts, to be sure. But the humanities are widely perceived as inessential, so it seems fine for them to be downsized, and for some departments to be eliminated completely. At one of our largest public universities, there has been talk recently of selecting a few humanities disciplines that are supposedly at the "core" of an undergraduate education, and eliminating the rest. The university's topnotch department of religious studies was informed that philosophy is part of the "core" but religious studies is not.[3] These changes are still under discussion, but they are typical of the sort of cost-cutting measures that are being contemplated in universities and colleges of many kinds. Even where cuts do not threaten whole departments, they threaten the health of departments, since faculty who cannot fill vacancies become overworked and are unable to do their job well.

To some extent, these threatening changes are externally imposed. We should not blame them all on outsiders, however. Too often, our universities have taken short-cuts—for example, by teaching large courses without sufficient critical engagement with students and without enough feedback on student writing; too often faculty allow regurgitation to lead to success. To the extent that universities fail to achieve the goals that I have defended, it becomes much easier for outsiders to depreciate humanistic studies.

The liberal arts, then, are threatened, both from without and from within. In a recent article, Harvard's president Drew Faust reports, and laments, "a steep decline in the percentage of students majoring in the liberal arts and sciences, and an accompanying increase in preprofessional undergraduate degrees." Have universities, she asks, "become too captive to the immediate and worldly purposes they serve? Has the market model become the fundamental and defining identity of higher education?" Faust concludes with a ringing defense of the liberal arts model and its role in our nation:

> Higher learning can offer individuals and societies a depth and breadth of vision absent from the inevitably myopic present. Human beings need meaning, understanding, and perspective as well as jobs. The question should not be whether we can afford to believe in such purposes in these times, but whether we can afford not to.[4]

Liberal arts education, then, is endangered in the United States, although it still has many strong defenders and a good chance of surviving. Outside the United States, many nations whose university curricula do not include a liberal arts component are now striving to build one, since they acknowledge its importance in crafting a public response to the problems of pluralism, fear, and suspicion their societies face. I've been involved in such discussions in the Netherlands, in Sweden, in India, in Germany, in Italy, and in Bangladesh. As I have observed, it is precisely in the Indian Institutes of Technology and Management—at the heart of the profit-oriented technology culture—that instructors have felt the need to introduce liberal arts courses, partly to counter the narrowness of their students, but partly, as well, to cope with religious- and caste-based animosities.

Whether much reform in this direction will occur, however, is hard to say, for liberal education has high financial and pedagogical costs. Teaching of the sort I recommend needs small classes, or at least sections, where students discuss ideas with one another, get copious feedback on frequent writing assignments, and have lots of time to discuss their work with instructors. European professors are not used to this idea, and would at present be horrible at it if they did try to do it, since their graduate education includes no training in teaching and this is not regarded as an important part of preparing their job file; in the United States, by contrast, graduate students are teaching assistants, frequently teach their own tutorials or small classes, and are supervised by faculty, since one all-important part of a job file is a "teaching portfolio," including professorial recommendations and student course evaluations. European faculty, lacking this systematic preparation, all too often come to expect that holding a chair means not having to grade undergraduate writing assignments. Graduate students, too, are often treated distantly and hierarchically.

Even when faculty are keen on the liberal arts model, bureaucrats are unwilling to believe that it is necessary to support the number of faculty positions required to make it really work. At Södertörn's Högskola, a new university in Stockholm where a high proportion of the students are immigrants, Vice-Chancellor Ingela Josefson wants to create a course called Democracy for all undergraduates, which would realize some of the goals of critical thinking and world citizenship that I have discussed here. She has sent young faculty to spend a year in liberal arts colleges in the United States so that they can learn the style of teaching that is needed to make this project work. Government bureaucrats, however, have so far refused to give the funding to create a course for all students that can be broken up into sections of twenty to twenty-five students. The course exists, but on a reduced level, not serving the needs of the entire student body. Meanwhile, an aggressive attempt to form partnerships with the various institutions for art education in Stockholm—schools that focus on theater, film study, dance, circus training, and music—is still in its infancy, and has not yet had the public support to influence the undergraduate curriculum at Södertörn.

Another problem that European and Asian universities have is that new disciplines of particular importance for good democratic citizenship have no secure place in the structure of undergraduate education. Women's studies, the study of race and ethnicity, Judaic studies, Islamic studies—all these are likely to be marginalized, catering only to the student who already knows a lot about the area and wants to focus on it. In the liberal arts system, by contrast, such new disciplines can provide courses that all undergraduates are required to take, and can also enrich the required liberal arts offerings in other disciplines, such as literature and history. Where there are no such requirements, the new disciplines remain marginal. I vividly remember attending a conference entitled "Religion and Violence against Women" sponsored by the women's studies program at Berlin's distinguished Humboldt University. The program was exciting, the topics urgent. Such a conference, at my own university, would probably have attracted almost 50 percent males, as my courses on topics such as feminist philosophy typically do. At Humboldt, however, apart from a few of the invited speakers, there was not a single male in the audience—with the exception of Sweden's ambassador to Germany, an old friend of mine whom I had invited. This is a typical experience in Europe, because the requirement to take a course on women's issues is often the only thing that destigmatizes the field for young men and makes it socially acceptable to show an interest in it.

Meanwhile, the pressure for economic growth has led many political leaders in Europe to recast the entirety of university education—both teaching and research—along growth-oriented lines, asking about the contribution of each discipline and each researcher to the economy. Take Britain, for example. Ever since the Thatcher era, it has been customary for humanities departments in Britain to be required to justify themselves to the government, which funds all academic institutions, by showing how their research and teaching contribute to economic profitability.[5] If they cannot show this, their government support will drop and the number of faculty and students decline. Whole departments may even be closed down, as numerous classics and philosophy programs have been. (British faculty do not have tenure any longer, so there is no barrier to firing them at any time; so far, though, the norm has been to transfer them to some nonclosed department until they retire.) These problems are closely related to the absence, in Britain and in Europe generally,[6] of a liberal arts model. Humanities departments cannot justify themselves by pointing to their role in teaching required liberal arts courses for all students, as they can in the United States.

Where departments are not closed, they are often merged these days with other units whose contribution to profit is more obvious—thus putting pressure on the merged discipline to emphasize those parts of its own scope that lie closer to profit, or can be made to seem to. When, for example, philosophy is merged with political science, it puts pressure on philosophy to focus on highly applied and "useful" areas, such as business ethics, rather than the study of Plato, or skills of logic and critical thinking, or reflections about the meaning of life—which might ultimately be more valuable in young people's attempts to understand themselves and their world. "Impact" is the buzzword of the day, and by "impact" the government clearly means above all economic impact.

Academic research, too, is increasingly driven by the demand for "impact." The current Labor government has recast all research, including humanities research, on the model of research in the sciences. It has to be supported by grant money, and researchers have to go out and find that money, usually from government bodies. Humanities research has not previously been funded in this way; it has traditionally been funded by stable direct funding because it has been understood that humanities research contributes to human life in a global way, not by producing this or that immediately useful discovery. Humanities professors in the United States get a certain amount of research leave as part of their standard contract. Typically they need to show that they are actively engaged in research and publication during that time, but they show this to peer faculty who understand what humanities research is about. British humanists have to continue filling out grant applications for government agencies, a great time killer, and also a great distorter of research topics, since the government agencies who screen grant applications are looking for "impact" and are often deeply suspicious of humanistic ideas. (Nor is Britain the most extreme in this regard. In some parts of Europe, one has to apply for a grant even to support one's own graduate students—who, in U.S. nonscience fields, and in many other countries as well, are funded by a standard agreement between an academic department and the university administration. Thus they can pursue their own education in an open-ended way, rather than being slotted into some professor's "research team" from the start.) One cynical young philosopher, in one of these recently merged departments of philosophy and political science, told me that his last grant proposal was six words under the word limit— so he added the word "empirical" six times, as if to reassure the bureaucrats that he was not dealing in mere philosophy—and his application proved successful.

These baneful trends have recently been formalized in a proposal by the Labor government for a new system of research assessment called the Research Excellence Framework. According to the new guidelines, fully 25 percent of the rating of a research proposal will depend on assessment of its "impact." Distinguished historian Stefan Collini has presented a devastating analysis of the scheme's likely impact on the humanities in "Impact on Humanities: Researchers Must Take a Stand Now or Be Judged and Rewarded as Salesmen." (He notes that responsibility for higher education in Britain is now part of the Department of Business, a dispiriting development.) Collini worries about the lack of protest against the cheapening vocabulary, which depicts research as a type of hucksterism: "Perhaps our ears no longer hear . . . how ludicrous it is to propose that the quality of scholarship can be partly judged in terms of the number of 'external research users' or the range of 'impact indicators.'" Academics in the humanities must insist, he argues, that their research is "a collection of ways of encountering the record of human activity in its greatest richness and diversity," and is valuable for this reason. If such a protest does not take place, humanists in Britain will devote more and more of their time "to becoming door-to-door salesmen for vulgarized versions of their increasingly market-oriented 'products.'"[7]

British humanists tell me that part of the problem is government's insensitivity to humanistic values when it assesses grant proposals; private foundations sometimes do better. Still, they feel, justly I believe, that the system of applying for grant money, though it may work well for the sciences, is not suited to the humanities and tends to corrupt the mission of humanistic scholarship. They consequently fear for the future of a humanities supported by no powerful public constituency. The British situation is typical of current developments in Europe.

In India the denigration of the humanities began long ago with Nehru's emphasis on science and economics as the linchpins of the nation's future. Despite his own deep love for poetry and literature, which informs every corner of his political analysis, Nehru concluded that modes of emotional and imaginative understanding must take a backseat to science, and his views prevailed.[8] Some humanities disciplines do not exist at all. Thus the study of comparative religion and the history of religions is not an academic subject in Indian universities. Other disciplines, such as philosophy, have long been weak and are stigmatized on that account; bright young people would not be encouraged to go into them, because "philosophy" has long been thought to mean something merely historical and linked to traditional religion, and is for this reason unpopular. The prestige disciplines are the sciences and engineering, economics, and to a certain extent empirical political science.

The hottest competition for entrance is for places in the Institutes of Technology and Management, where (apart from the required humanities general-education courses that have wisely been introduced) only technical education is on offer. A prominent research scientist of Indian origin at my own university—himself educated at IIT Delhi—described the whole IIT experience as one of "de-education," in the sense that students focus narrowly on preprofessional skills and are discouraged from learning independent research techniques. Moreover, he emphasized, this narrowing begins far earlier. Since entrance to the IITs is by nationwide competitive examination, the victorious students are from towns all over the country. Most have been raised to think that getting a good job is the main aim of education. The idea that people should learn things that prepare them to be active, thoughtful citizens is an idea that has "never crossed their path." As I have mentioned, and my science colleague agrees, the humanities courses—which students actually enjoy—supply a temporary and partial corrective to the narrowness of the rest of the education, but, given the overall structure of incentives in the students' situation, their effect is rarely lasting.

What of the interdisciplinary university that Tagore created, called "All-the-World"? Visva-Bharati was running short of money, so it turned to the government for help. The price of financial support was a loss of independence, and Visva-Bharati rapidly lost its distinctive liberal arts curriculum. Now it is a university like every other, only with somewhat lower standards than many.

Although this is not my topic, we in the United States should pause at this point to be thankful for our traditions, which combine a liberal arts model with a strong cultivation of humanistic philanthropy and a basically private-endowment structure of funding. (Even the stronger U.S. state systems, such as the University of Michigan and the University of California, are increasingly relying on private endowment money.) We did not deliberate and wisely choose this system, but we can be happy that it has evolved and that we can all rely on it.

At my own university, for example, we do not have to go hat in hand to bureaucrats who lack all sympathy with what we do. Instead, we go to wealthy alums whose educational values pretty well match our own since they are by and large alums who loved their undergraduate liberal arts education, whatever else they went on to do. They love the life of the mind, and they want others to enjoy it. It would not be easy for another country to arrive at our system, because ours rests on broad-based liberal arts education at the undergraduate level, with lots of individual attention from faculty—something people value and want to pass on to future generations—and also on tax incentives for charitable donation and a long-established culture of philanthropy. Building such a system, if another country wanted to do it, would take many years. (Britain is now trying, but it is unclear how far the effort will succeed.) We in the United States can be grateful for our good luck, since our politicians are no more friendly to the humanities than those of other nations.

Even here, in what might seem to be a secure bastion of the humanities, there are signs of trouble. A recent controversy here at the University of Chicago concerns the fact that the Viewbook for prospective students has been revised to show lots of students in gleaming laboratories, and no students sitting and thinking. Campus tours, too, have apparently been instructed to bypass the traditional bastions of humanistic learning to focus on parts of the campus associated with medicine, science, and preprofessional studies.[9] Apparently someone thinks that our undergraduate programs will look more attractive if they are represented as less focused on philosophy, literature, history, and other subjects that have traditionally been staples of our core curriculum.

The universities of the world have great merits, then, but also great problems. They are far from preparing young people for citizenship as well as they might, although some still do a very good job.

By contrast, training for citizenship is doing poorly in every nation in the most crucial years of children's lives, those known as K through 12, where the demands of the global market have made everyone focus on scientific and technical proficiencies as *the* key abilities, and the humanities and the arts are increasingly perceived as useless frills that we can prune away to make sure our nation (whether it be India or the United States) remains competitive. To the extent that the humanities and arts are the focus of national discussion, they are recast as technical abilities that ought to be tested by quantitative multiple-choice examinations, and the imaginative and critical abilities that lie at their core are typically left aside.

In the United States, national testing (under the No Child Left Behind Act [NCLB]) has already made things worse, as national testing usually does, for critical thinking and sympathetic imagining are not testable by quantitative multiple-choice exams, and the skills involved in world citizenship are also poorly tested in such a way. (Consider how world history would have to be assessed on a standardized test; all that I have said about learning to examine evidence, criticize a historical narrative, and think critically about differences among narratives would have to be omitted.) "Teaching to the test," which increasingly dominates public school classrooms, produces an atmosphere of student passivity and teacher routinization. The creativity and individuality that mark the best humanistic teaching and learning has a hard time finding room to unfold. When testing determines a school's entire future, forms of student-teacher exchange that do not have a payoff on tests are likely to be squeezed out. Whether a nation is aspiring, like India, to a greater share of the market, or struggling to protect jobs, like the United States, the imagination and the critical faculties look like useless paraphernalia, and people even have increasing contempt for them. Across the board, the curriculum is being stripped of its humanistic elements, and the pedagogy of rote learning rules the roost.

Notice that part of the issue here is content, and part is pedagogy. Curricular content has shifted away from material that focuses on enlivening imagination and training the critical faculties toward material that is directly relevant to test preparation. Along with the shift in content has come an even more baneful shift in pedagogy: away from teaching that seeks to promote questioning and individual responsibility toward force-feeding for good exam results.

The No Child Left Behind Act was prompted by a real problem; we have tremendous inequalities in our schools. Some children get vastly greater educational opportunities than others. What should we do, if we think that we need national assessment in order to promote greater educational equality, but reject the current form of national assessment for the reasons I have given? It is not impossible to create a nuanced, qualitative form of national assessment. Indeed, the United States had the ingredients for one in previous years, and an excellent recent book about accountability, Richard Rothstein's *Grading Education: Getting Accountability Right*, proposes a multilayered state and federal program that tests a variety of cognitive and behavioral outcomes in a far more sophisticated way than NCLB, focusing in particular on skills needed for good citizenship.[10] This sensible and well-argued book is an excellent starting point for a really helpful national debate about accountability.

Although I have just criticized the British approach to the humanities at the university level, it seems clear that in the high schools the British have done better with assessment than we have.[11] The GCSE (formerly O-level) and A-level exams that students take in a variety of subjects in their high school years are essay exams read by multiple readers and graded the way one would grade a student paper. Philosophy is one of the high school subjects that is rapidly growing in popularity, and philosophers seem to agree that it is not some terrible travesty of philosophy that is tested (for example, facts about the lives and "doctrines" of famous philosophers), it is really Socratic philosophical ability: the ability to analyze and think critically about a wide range of philosophical issues. In other areas, similarly, testing is ambitious and qualitative. So testing can be good, preserving humanistic values. If good teachers know how to grade their students' work in class, there can be a test devised to measure what is graded. The only problem is that this sort of testing will be much more expensive than the standardized type, and we will have to devote a lot of attention to recruiting a competent bunch of assessors and paying them well, something that nobody currently seems willing even to discuss.

The Obama administration has a chance to change the current modus operandi, promoting a richer conception of education and, if desired, a richer, more qualitative conception of testing. President Obama's own personal values would seem to lead toward supporting such changes; he is famous for his interest in hearing and sifting the arguments on all sides of an issue, and he declares his great interest in "empathy" as a characteristic pertinent to an office as high as that of Justice of the U.S. Supreme Court. His own education clearly had the characteristics I have been praising here, and it produced a person who knows how to think critically, who thinks with rich information about a wide range of world situations, who repeatedly displays a robust ability to imagine the predicaments of many types of people—and its corollary, the ability to think reflectively about himself and his own life story. Very likely, Barack Obama's home life contributed a great deal to this process, but his schools must have done their part. And we know that when the time came for college, he attended two institutions famous for their commitment to the liberal arts model: Occidental, a fine liberal arts college, and Columbia University, where the undergraduate humanities curriculum is well known for its comprehensiveness and for the engaged, enterprising teaching with which material is presented.

Nonetheless, so far at least, President Obama has not given any signals of support for the humanities or a reform of national education efforts in a liberal arts direction. His choice for secretary of education, Arne Duncan, inspires no confidence, since as head of the Chicago public schools Duncan presided over a rapid decline in humanities and arts funding. And the indications are that rather than decreasing the focus on the type of national testing pioneered under No Child Left Behind, the administration plans to expand it. In his speeches on education, the president rightly emphasizes the issue of equality, talking about the importance of making all Americans capable of pursuing the "American Dream." But the pursuit of a dream requires dreamers: educated minds that can think critically about alternatives and imagine an ambitious goal—preferably not involving only personal or even national wealth, but involving human dignity and democratic debate as well.

Instead of such important and generous goals, however, President Obama has so far focused on individual income and national economic progress, arguing that the sort of education we need is the sort that serves these two goals. "[E]conomic progress and educational achievement have always gone hand in hand in America," he insists. We should judge any new idea in education by how well it "works"—presumably with reference to these goals. He defends early childhood interventions by saying, "For every dollar we invest in these programs, we get nearly ten dollars back in reduced welfare rolls, fewer health care costs, and less crime." Never in this entire lengthy speech does he mention the democratic goals I have emphasized. And when he mentions critical thinking—once—it is in the context of what businesses need for profitability. We need, he says, to develop tests that measure "whether they possess 21st century skills like problem-solving and critical thinking, entrepreneurship and creativity." This one gesture toward the humanities—in a speech largely devoted to the praise of science and technology—is clearly a narrow allusion to the role of certain skills in business advancement. And the proposed assessment—a strengthened form of NCLB—shows very clearly that the humanistic parts of the sentence are not the core of the proposal.[12]

Even more problematic, President Obama repeatedly praises nations of the Far East, for example Singapore, which, in his view, have advanced beyond us in technology and science education. And he praises such nations in an ominous manner: "They are spending less time teaching things that don't matter, and more time teaching things that do. They are preparing their students not only for high school or college, but for a career. We are not." In other words, "things that matter" is taken to be equivalent to "things that prepare for a career." A life of rich significance and respectful, attentive citizenship is nowhere mentioned among the goals worth spending time on. In the context of his speech, it is difficult to avoid the conclusion that the "things that don't matter" include many of the things that this book has defended as essential to the health of democracy.[13]

The U.S. system of public education contains huge inequalities. It is tempting to think that national testing offers a solution to this problem. Nonetheless, one does not solve the problem of unequal opportunity through a type of testing that virtually ensures that no child has the opportunity for a stimulating education or adequate preparation for citizenship.

What of India? I have spoken of India's disdain for humanistic content at the university level. Very much the same is true of elementary and secondary schools, since these are heavily influenced by prevailing social norms and national trends. Tagore's school in Santiniketan still exists, but, as we saw, its focus on the arts makes it very unfashionable in the present climate. Once a highly sought-after destination for the most talented students from all over India—Nehru's daughter Indira passed her only truly happy years of schooling there, for example—it is now stigmatized as a place for problem children, and parents are not proud to send a child there. Such a school does not offer the type of preparation that is likely to lead to success in the IIT entrance examination. At those same Institutes of Technology and Management, meanwhile, instructors lament their students' deficient humanities preparation.

Humanistic content, then, is in decline—from a position that was already insecure. What of pedagogy? Throughout the nation, the pedagogy of rote learning has dominated for many decades. It is in a sense not surprising that a nation struggling to produce mass literacy from a position of low literacy would focus on drilling and would neglect the empowerment of the individual student through questioning, sifting of evidence, and imaginative expression. Such a result is even more understandable when we remember that rote learning dominated in colonial times. The schools that Tagore briefly attended and rapidly left all utilized this sort of boring cramming, and it was this that motivated him to try to create something different. But to understand is not to condone. Again and again I have heard Indian Americans express regret about the stultifying quality of their own education, by contrast to the good things they observe in the schools their children attend.

Rote learning dominates, then, in government schools. So too do many forms of corruption; in some states the teacher absenteeism rate is as high as 20 percent.[14] Equally damaging to children is the infamous practice of "private tuition," where teachers accept a fee to teach well-off kids in their homes after school—a practice that creates incentives not to teach well during the normal school day. Teachers all too rarely try to innovate, to inspire children. Their highest hope is to stuff them full of facts so that they perform well on national examinations.

Ironically, such bad practices dominate in the very places—government elementary and secondary schools—where we would suppose that students, being at least in school and, after a while, literate, have already had relatively good luck and seem to have a realistic hope of attaining an influential position in society. (Literacy rates in the nation as a whole still hover around 50 percent for women, 65 percent for men, so anyone who progresses even to secondary education is privileged.) At the "bottom" of society, however, something more promising is often on offer. Thousands of rural literacy programs funded by nongovernmental organizations teach basic literacy and basic skills. The ones I know well focus on women and girls, but such programs come in many varieties. What many of them have in common, however, is resourcefulness and imagination. Working women and girls will not come to class unless they get something out of it, and so teachers are forced to be innovative, warm, experimental. They use drawing, dance, and music; they involve students in mapping and talking about the power structure of their village, or in reflecting about how they might get a better deal from the landlords for whom they work as sharecroppers. They communicate excitement about what they are doing, something that few government teachers manage to do.

What these programs show us is that improving the bleak situation of the arts and humanities requires, above all, human investment. Money is nice, but committed people, and strong support for such programs, are the main factors.

We in the United States can study our own future in the government schools of India. Such will be our future *if* we continue down the road of "teaching to the test," neglecting the activities that enliven children's minds and make them see a connection between their school life and their daily life outside of school. We should be deeply alarmed that our own schools are rapidly, heedlessly, moving in the direction of the Indian norm, rather than the reverse.

DURING THE ERA in which people began to demand democratic self-governance, education all over the world was remodeled to produce the sort of student who could function well in this demanding form of government: not a cultivated gentleman, stuffed with the wisdom of the ages, but an active, critical, reflective, and empathetic member of a community of equals, capable of exchanging ideas on the basis of respect and understanding with people from many different backgrounds. Rousseau, Pestalozzi, Froebel, Alcott, and Tagore differed in many ways, but they all agreed that the passive pedagogy of the past offered little to the nations of the future, that a new sense of personal agency and a new critical freedom would be needed if participatory institutions were to be sustained.

Today we still maintain that we like democracy and self-governance, and we also think that we like freedom of speech, respect for difference, and understanding of others. We give these values lip service, but we think far too little about what we need to do in order to transmit them to the next generation and ensure their survival. Distracted by the pursuit of wealth, we increasingly ask our schools to turn out useful profit-makers rather than thoughtful citizens. Under pressure to cut costs, we prune away just those parts of the educational endeavor that are crucial to preserving a healthy society.

What will we have, if these trends continue? Nations of technically trained people who do not know how to criticize authority, useful profit-makers with obtuse imaginations. As Tagore observed, a suicide of the soul. What could be more frightening than that? Indeed, when we consider the Indian state of Gujarat, which has for a particularly long time gone down this road, with no critical thinking in the public schools and a concerted focus on technical ability, we can see clearly how a band of docile engineers can be welded into a murderous force to enact the most horrendously racist and antidemocratic policies. (In 2002 Hindu right-wing mobs, egged on by propaganda purveyed in the schools—Hitler, for example, is portrayed as a hero in state history textbooks—murdered approximately 2,000 Muslim civilians, a genocidal assault that has been condemned around the world and has led to the denial of a U.S. visa to that state's chief minister, who masterminded the whole campaign of religious hatred.[15]) And yet, how can we possibly avoid going down this road?

DEMOCRACIES HAVE GREAT rational and imaginative powers. They also are prone to some serious flaws in reasoning, to parochialism, haste, sloppiness, selfishness, narrowness of the spirit. Education based mainly on profitability in the global market magnifies these deficiencies, producing a greedy obtuseness and a technically trained docility that threaten the very life of democracy itself, and that certainly impede the creation of a decent world culture.

If the real clash of civilizations is, as I believe, a clash within the individual soul, as greed and narcissism contend against respect and love, all modern societies are rapidly losing the battle, as they feed the forces that lead to violence and dehumanization and fail to feed the forces that lead to cultures of equality and respect. If we do not insist on the crucial importance of the humanities and the arts, they will drop away, because they do not make money. They only do what is much more precious than that, make a world that is worth living in, people who are able to see other human beings as full people, with thoughts and feelings of their own that deserve respect and empathy, and nations that are able to overcome fear and suspicion in favor of sympathetic and reasoned debate.

NOTES

I. The Silent Crisis

1. *A Test of Leadership: Charting the Future of U.S. Higher Education*, available online. A valuable counterreport is *College Learning for the New Global Century*, issued by the National Leadership Council for Liberal Education and America's Promise (LEAP), a group organized by the Association of American Colleges and Universities (Washington, DC, 2007), with whose recommendations I am largely in agreement (not surprisingly, in that I participated in drafting it).

2. I first explored these abilities in *Citizens of the World: A Classical Defense of Reform in Liberal Education* (Cambridge, MA: Harvard University Press, 1997), a book concerned only with developments in higher education in the United States, and with just the required "general education" portion of higher education.

3. One valuable project that focuses on these ingredients in basic science education is Project Kaleidoscope, www.pkal.org.

4. On education and flourishing lives, see Harry Brighouse, *On Education* (New York: Routledge, 2006); the LEAP report (above, n. 1); and the related discussion of self-development in Kwame Anthony Appiah, *The Ethics of Identity* (Princeton: Princeton University Press, 2005).

II. Education for Profit, Education for Democracy

1. This has been shown with particular clarity by Jean Drèze and Amartya Sen in *India: Development and Participation* (New York and Oxford: Oxford University Press, 2002), and in the earlier edition, which has the title *India: Social Development and Economic Opportunity* (New York and

Oxford: Oxford University Press, 1996). The data come from studies of different Indian states that have adopted different policies, some favoring economic growth without direct support for health and education, some favoring direct government action to support health and education (which the Indian Constitution leaves to the states). The field studies are gathered in Drèze and Sen, editors, *Indian Development: Selected Regional Perspectives* (Delhi, New York, and Oxford: Oxford University Press, 1997).

2. See Drèze and Sen, *India: Development and Participation.*

3. Jobs in health and education are under state control according to the Indian Constitution, so the national government can affect development in these areas only indirectly.

4. Article 21 of the Indian Constitution speaks only of "life and liberty," but "life" has since been interpreted to mean "life commensurate with human dignity." The South African Constitution has gone much further, however, in giving constitutional form to basic welfare rights.

5. Rabindranath Tagore, *Nationalism* (New York: Macmillan, 1917).

6. See Nussbaum, *The Clash Within: Democracy, Religious Violence, and India's Future* (Cambridge, MA: Harvard University Press, 2007), ch. 8, for a detailed account, with references and citations.

7. See Nussbaum, "Violence on the Left: Nandigram and the Communists of West Bengal," *Dissent*, Spring 2008, 27–33.

8. Thus, in West Bengal, it was the arts community that earliest and most strongly opposed government policies of kicking rural laborers off their land without skills training or job opportunities; see ibid.

III. Educating Citizens: The Moral (and Anti-Moral) Emotions

1. The history of the Indo-European languages shows us that Hindus almost certainly migrated into India from outside. (If there were any truly indigenous people, these were the Dravidian people of southern India.) Muslims and Christians arrived from outside, later, in small numbers, but the bulk of contemporary Indian Muslims and Christians are converts from Hinduism. In any case, the idea that the date of one's arrival in a place— 1500 B.C.E., say, rather than 1600 C.E.—gives one a claim to more citizenship rights should be vigorously rejected.

2. See my discussion of televised versions of the *Mahabharata* and *Ramayana* in *The Clash Within*, ch. 5. For a totally different use of the *Mahabharata* for purposes of contemporary social reflection, see Gurcharan Das's wonderful book, *The Difficulty of Being Good: On the Subtle Art of Dharma* (Delhi: Penguin, 2009; London: Penguin, 2010; and New York: Oxford University Press, 2010). Das is profiled in chapter 2 of my *The Clash Within*.

3. I argue for this account in detail in Nussbaum, *Upheavals of Thought: The Intelligence of Emotions* (Cambridge: Cambridge University Press, 2001), ch. 4.

4. For a more extensive analysis of both shame and disgust, see Nussbaum, *Hiding from Humanity: Disgust, Shame, and the Law* (Princeton: Princeton University Press, 2004).

5. See the references in ibid. to the experimental work of Paul Rozin, Jonathan Haidt, and others.

6. Rozin's experiments make clear the gap between disgust and the sense of danger.

7. See *Hiding*, chs. 2 and 4. My psychological account owes a large debt to the concepts and arguments of Donald Winnicott.

8. Did the beloved story of Hansel and Gretel, made fashionable in the opera by Humperdinck, himself a disciple of Wagner, who sought to extol the pure German *Volk*, contribute to fantasies that led, later, to the perhaps unconscious selection of a mode of extermination? At the opera's end, the blond German children come to life, freed from the witch's spell, and cheer her incineration.

9. See Frans de Waal, *Good Natured: The Origins of Right and Wrong in Humans and Other Animals* (Cambridge, MA: Harvard University Press, 1996).

10. C. Daniel Batson, *The Altruism Question* (Hillsdale, NJ: Lawrence Erlbaum, 1991).

11. See Dale J. Langford, Sara E. Crager, Zarrar Shehzad, Shad B. Smith, Susana G. Sotocinal, Jeremy S. Levenstadt, Mona Lisa Chanda, Daniel J. Levitin, and Jeffrey S. Mogil, "Social Modulation of Pain as Evidence for Empathy in Mice," *Science* 312 (2006), 1967–70.

12. See Candace Clark, *Misery and Company: Sympathy in Everyday Life* (Chicago: University of Chicago Press, 1997).

13. Dan Kindlon and Michael Thompson, *Raising Cain: Protecting the Emotional Life of Boys* (New York: Ballantine, 1999).

14. For a concise summary of Milgram's and Asch's research, see Philip Zimbardo, *The Lucifer Effect: How Good People Turn Evil* (London: Rider, 2007), 260–75.

15. Christopher R. Browning, *Ordinary Men: Reserve Police Battalion 101 and the Final Solution in Poland* (New York: HarperCollins, 1993).

16. Reported in Zimbardo, *The Lucifer Effect*, 283–85.

17. See my review of Zimbardo, *Times Literary Supplement*, October 10, 2007, 3–5.

18. Again, my summary is based on a wide range of research described in Zimbardo.

IV. Socratic Pedagogy: The Importance of Argument

1. See Nussbaum, *Cultivating Humanity: A Classical Defense of Reform in Liberal Education* (Cambridge, MA: Harvard University Press, 1997), ch. 1.

2. Malcolm Gladwell, *Outliers: The Study of Success* (New York: Little, Brown, and Co., 2008).

3. See *Cultivating Humanity*, chs. 1 and 8.

4. See Dewey, "Froebel's Educational Principles," in *The School and Society and The Child and the Curriculum* (Chicago: University of Chicago Press, 1990), 116–31.

5. Dewey, *The School and Society*, 112–15.

6. See ibid., 20–22, where Dewey shows how many complex historical, economic, and scientific ideas can be elicited from the apparently simple task of producing cotton thread.

7. Ibid., 19.

8. See Nussbaum, "Land of My Dreams: Islamic Liberalism under Fire in India," *Boston Review* 34 (March/April 2009), 10–14.

9. See Kathleen M. O'Connell, *Rabindranath Tagore: The Poet as Educator* (Kolkata: Visva-Bharati, 2002).

10. *Auguste Comte and Positivism* (London: Westminster Review, 1865).

11. Translated in V. Bhatia, ed., *Rabindranath Tagore: Pioneer in Educa-*

tion (New Delhi: Sahitya Chayan, 1994). All references in the rest of the chapter are to this translation.

12. Cited by O'Connell, *Rabindranath Tagore*.

13. Maria Montessori (1870–1952), a great educator, follower of Pestalozzi and in conversation with Tagore, made such minute prescriptions for the conduct of the school day that the worldwide educational movement she inspired has to some extent been hampered by the degree of guidance she offered and the sense of authority she imposed.

14. See Gareth Matthews, *Philosophy and the Young Child* (Cambridge, MA: Harvard University Press, 1982), and *Dialogues with Children* (Cambridge, MA: Harvard University Press, 1984).

15. Matthew Lipman, *Harry Stottlemeier's Discovery* (Montclair, NJ: Institute for the Advancement of Philosophy for Children, 1982), 1–14.

16. M. Lipman, A. M. Sharp, and F. S. Oscanyan, *Philosophy in the Classroom* (Philadelphia: Temple University Press, 1980).

V. Citizens of the World

1. O'Connell, *Rabindranath Tagore*, 148.

2. Amita Sen, *Joy in All Work* (Kolkata: Bookfront Publication Forum, 1999).

3. O'Connell, *Rabindranath Tagore*, 148.

4. John Dewey, *Democracy and Education* (New York: Macmillan, 1916, reprinted Mineola, NY: Dover, 2004), 207.

5. Dewey, *The School and Society*, 89, 11, 15, 24.

6. See Nussbaum, *The Clash Within*, ch. 7.

7. For a detailed analysis of specific passages, see Nussbaum, *The Clash Within*, ch. 7.

8. See www.fpspi.org.

9. Conversation with D. Parthasarathy, March 2008 (at a conference in Delhi on affirmative action in higher education).

VI. Cultivating Imagination: Literature and the Arts

1. See Nussbaum, *Cultivating Humanity*, ch. 3.

2. See F. Robert Rodman, *Winnicott: Life and Work* (Cambridge, MA: Perseus Publishing, 2003).

3. Donald Winnicott, *Playing and Reality* (London and New York: Routledge, 2005, originally published 1971).

4. See Nussbaum, *Poetic Justice: The Literary Imagination and Public Life* (Boston: Beacon, 1995), ch. 1.

5. See Rodman's extensive discussion. For Guntrip's analysis with Winnicott, see J. Hazell, *H.J.S. Guntrip: A Psychoanalytical Biography* (London: Free Association Books, 1986).

6. Donald Winnicott, *Holding and Interpretation: Fragments of an Analysis* (New York: Grove Press, 1986), 95.

7. Dewey, *Democracy and Education*, 226, 227.

8. Amita Sen, *Joy in All Work*.

9. Ibid., 35.

10. Ralph Ellison, *Invisible Man* (New York: Random House, 1992 Modern Library edition, with Introduction by Ellison, added 1981; originally published 1952), Introduction.

11. On the use of play and the arts by the Hindu right, see Nussbaum, *The Clash Within*.

12. Johann Gottfried Herder, "Letters for the Advancement of Humanity" (1793–97), translated by Michael Forster, in Forster, ed., *Herder: Philosophical Writings* (Cambridge: Cambridge University Press, 2002), Letter 119, 404–409.

13. See arguments and references in the LEAP Report, *College Learning for the New Global Century*.

14. See discussion in Richard Rothstein, with Rebecca Jacobsen and Tamara Wilder, *Grading Education: Getting Accountability Right* (Washington, DC: Economic Policy Institute, 2008), 18.

VII. Democratic Education on the Ropes

1. Focusing only on the arts and only on pre-college education in the United States, good summaries of trends can be found in the CNN.com article "Budgets Cut Student Experience," http://www.cnn.com/2003/

EDUCATION/08/13/sprj.sch.cuts/, discussing the effects of the No Child Left Behind Act. See also "Cuts in Arts Programs Leave Sour Note in Schools," http://www.weac.org/news_and_publications/at_the_capitol/archives/2003-2004/arts.aspx. For the drastic impact of the California budget crisis on music and art (which are basically gone), see "L.A. Schools Budget Cut, 2,000 Teachers Gone," http://www.npr.org/templates/story/story.php?storId=105848204.

2. See Nussbaum, *Cultivating Humanity*.

3. Personal conversation with religion faculty at Arizona State University, March 2009.

4. "The University's Crisis of Purpose," *New York Times Book Review*, September 6, 2009, 19.

5. One part of this shift, but only one, is the mandatory research and teaching assessment, which measures faculty research and teaching effectiveness in mechanical ways (number of pages, whether the instructor uses PowerPoint, and so forth). The more insidious aspect is the demand—once implicit, now quite open—that research be shown to have "impact," meaning contribution to national economic goals.

6. Scotland used to have a four-year B.A. degree, with the first year devoted to liberal arts courses. The commitment of Scottish universities to the liberal arts was famous even in the nineteenth century: John Stuart Mill's Inaugural Lecture at the University of St. Andrews praises the suitability of the Scottish university system for democratic citizenship, by contrast with England's narrower curriculum, focused on theology. The standardization of higher education imposed by the EU's Bologna scheme, however, has made Scotland assimilate to the rest of Europe, rather than vice versa.

7. *Times Literary Supplement*, November 13, 2009, 18–19.

8. For Nehru's ambivalence about the humanities, see Nussbaum, "Nehru, Religion, and the Humanities," in Wendy Doniger and Martha Nussbaum, *India: Implementing Pluralism and Democracy* (New York: Oxford University Press, forthcoming 2010).

9. "Tour Guides Take Route Less Traveled," *Chicago Maroon*, October 16, 2009. The "apparently" in my text is there because the *Maroon*, a student newspaper, is not always totally accurate, but the data it presents are convincing.

10. Rothstein, *Grading Education*. For the earlier assessment model, in the National Assessment of Educational Progress (NAEP) in the 1950s and 1960s, see ch. 6.

11. For other aspects of the British assessment system, see Rothstein, *Grading Education*, ch. 7.

12. Barack Obama's speech on education, *Wall Street Journal* blog, March 10, 2009.

13. Ibid.

14. See *The Pratichi Education Report: The Delivery of Primary Education, a Study in West Bengal*, by the Pratichi Research Team, Kumar Rana, Abdur Rafique, Amrita Sengupta, with an introduction by Amartya Sen, no. 1 (2002) (Delhi: TLM Books, 2002).

15. See Nussbaum, *The Clash Within*, especially chs. 1 and 9.

INDEX

The Public Square Book Series
PRINCETON UNIVERSITY PRESS

With Thanks to the Donors of the Public Square

President William P. Kelly,
the CUNY Graduate Center

President Jeremey Travis,
John Jay College of Criminal Justice

Myron S. Glucksman

Caroline Urvater